Anatomy of Marriage

Anatomy of Marriage

Minard Alvaro McAlister

VANTAGE PRESS
New York

Cover design by Susan Thomas

FIRST EDITION

Published by Vantage Press, Inc.
419 Park Ave. South, New York, NY 10016

Manufactured in the United States of America
ISBN: 978-0-533-15908-6

Library of Congress Catalog Card No.: 2007906817

0 9 8 7 6 5 4 3 2 1

To my wife, Mary Terrell McAlister

But words are things, and a small drop of ink,
Falling like dew, upon a thought, produces
That which makes thousands, perhaps millions, think.

—*Don Juan,* Lord Byron

Contents

Prologue

I am a lawyer. This work evolved from the practice of domestic law (divorces, child custody, etc.).

When I began the practice of law in the mid-fifties, the state in which I am practicing had finally permitted divorce a few years earlier, even though most of the states within the Union had had divorce legislation for years. The legislation limited the grounds for divorce to adultery, physical cruelty and habitual drunkenness. Normally, any legislation that totally changes things takes a few years to become acceptable. But I am in the Bible Belt, so it took nearly twenty years for divorce to become socially acceptable. Between the fifties and the mid-sixties, divorces were just a trickle, and I had an interview for divorce, on an average, of probably three (3) a month—only the more enlightened were divorced. During this period, most divorces were filed by women, and most of the women (with children in a majority of cases) had lived for a number of years in an environment in which they had been either physically abused, or threatened with physical abuse, but, yet, these instances of abuse seemed to be isolated events.

Beginning in the late sixties, there was a rush to divorce, even in the Bible Belt, in all of society: all economic strata, all educational levels, all ethnic groups, the heterosexual, homosexual, perverted, neurotic, fanatic, submissive, arrogant, religious, atheist, professional, white-collar, blue-collar, skilled, semi-skilled, etc.

Again, the women, generally speaking, were the ones to file and the ground most often was physical cruelty or habitual drunkenness (these grounds usually go together). After the "rush" began, it was not unusual to have three (3) interviews in one day, mostly with women. With this many interviews, it did not take long to show the facts in all were basically the same, only the names changed. It became obvious that the number of women who were living in an environment in which they were being, or had been, either physically abused, or threatened with physical abuse, or subjected to personal degradation, emotional uncertainty, servitude, embarrassment, humiliation, financial debauchery, neglect, aloneness, or several combinations of, and, in the extreme case, all of these (with children in a majority of cases) was of epidemic proportion.

Early in the practice, I discovered that the best way to find out if there was some chance to save a marriage, with a meaningful relationship, was to find out the woman's feelings during the sexual relation. The feeling of the woman during the sexual relation was a barometer as to whether, generally, the marriage could be saved with a meaningful relationship. I refer to the feeling of the woman because for most men a sexual relation is nothing more than a sexual relation—a spasm of the genitals.

When the woman was asked, "Why did you stay with your husband so long?" with few exceptions, the answer would be, "Because I still love him."

Yet, when she was asked, "What was your feeling during a sexual relation?" most responded, "I try to avoid it." When pressed for an answer, again, with few exceptions, her answer would be, "It's a wifely duty," or "I felt I had to," "Awful" or "Disgust," "You hope it will be over soon," or some similar answer that told it was not pleasurable.

The answers were, obviously, inconsistent with "love"; one does not feel revulsion in a sexual act with one who is loved. It was obvious, in most of the cases, the relationship between the parties was artificial. There was no mutual respect, mutual desire to be with one another, mutual unrestrained cooperation and honesty (all of the vital aspects of a meaningful relationship), and such had been missing for a long time before the divorce was filed. In fact, these marriages reminded me of the life support machine used by the medical profession for people in which all vital signs (brain waves, blood pressure, breathing, etc.) have ceased. Life, while on this machine, is artificial; it (life) is "form" without "substance." So, too, were these marriages, "form" (union) without "substance" (a meaningful relationship), with an abusive and hostile environment. And those filing for a divorce were only the "tip of the iceberg."

Too, I began to notice the manner in which the child, or children, were disciplined by the clients during the interviews. I was astounded. Over a period of time, the manner in which the children were disciplined almost fell into patterns. The children were either:

ignored—child could do anything it wanted to, including marking or hitting wall, running through office crying, yelling, lying on floor crying or getting into everything which required secretary to get involved;

bribed or appeased—child was given soft drinks, candy, cookies, chewing gum (all of which were handy) or promised the moon;

or **slapped, spanked, hit, jerked or threatened with some future retaliation or bodily harm.**

I cannot remember an incident in the office in which the child was treated in a mature fashion, there were so few. I appreciated the fact that the client was under considerable stress, under the circumstances, and, psychologically, made an allowance for such. However, I, also, became more aware of how children were treated by their parents when I was out in public, such as the Mall. Not surprising, I observed the treatment of the children to be much the same. Since the age of the parents, generally, in the office and public observation, ranged from teenager to about thirty years, I concluded the discipline used was the same kind of discipline these parents had been subjected to when growing up. I came to this conclusion as it seemed to me the discipline given was out of frustration, and spontaneous, rather than a rational decision. But, these statements are not intended to be critical. The obvious frustration the parents suffered seemed to arise out of a sense of being unable to cope with the situation; in other words, they simply did not know what to do.

The magnitude of the number of women, with children in most cases, who had lived so long in an abusive and hostile environment made me wonder *how* and *why*. Since the relationship (bond between man and woman) is far more important, generally speaking, to the woman than the man, how did these women remain in such a relationship for a number of years, especially since the children were, also, being brutalized, physically and psychologically? Why did husbands abuse their wives and children?

What was the "support system" by which these marriages continued to function when all vital aspects of a meaningful relationship were dead?

It occurred to me that as knowledge had been gained from dead bodies for the causes of death, so too, knowledge could be gained from dead relationships (divorces) for the causes of divorce. The doctor has a cadaver that gives him access to all the organs of the body. In the process of a divorce, the lawyer has access to the client's thoughts, feelings, aspirations, intimacies, motivations and fears in the relationship. While most associate the word "autopsy" with the examination of a dead body to determine the cause of death, another meaning is seeing with one's own eyes, witnessing, personal observation and inspection. A law office can afford the same environment for investigation as a laboratory; there is opportunity for personal observation and inspection. The lawyer hears both sides of a divorce; one side is heard in his office, the other side is heard during the trial. With this information, every divorce was an opportunity to gain knowledge about the reasons for the failure of marriage. Any quest for answers begins at the core of ignorance with search for information. As information is accumulated, patterns form; as patterns form, conclusions are drawn and theories are constructed. Theories and conclusions are tested and, then, accepted or rejected from results. By questions, observation, comparison of facts, and reasoning, the essence of the phenomena of violence in the family (society) could be found. A study—posteriori (from the effect to the cause)—could be made.

In the interview with the client, in addition to the usual questions about the marriage, I began to ask questions that would shed some light on the *why* and *how*.

This study began in earnest in the seventies and ultimately included over 2,000 families. When the study began, I reviewed many of the early files to see if they fit into the same pattern as the current files. They did. Any one of the old files of divorce, handled prior to 1970, could have been a current file. The institution of marriage had not changed.

Unexpectedly, I became aware that observing and probing marriages was as though you were looking at society under a microscope; the institution of marriage and society were one and the same.

Domestic practice made manifest that the relationship of man-woman, alone, is of little significance. They are adults and have the right to maintain their lifestyle in any manner they choose, even if there is brutality in that relationship, so long as it does not interfere with or hurt someone else.

But, when a child enters the picture, there is "family." And, "family" must be synonymous with "children" or it has no meaning; otherwise, relationships—marriages—civilizations without children would expire rapidly.

It is man\woman in an intimate relationship (regardless of whether a civil or religious marriage ceremony has taken place) that transmit to the child of that relationship the essential characteristics of male and female, and the psychological atmosphere (mores) of the society just by being a part of that society. That which I was taught in college was now understood: the individual family (man-woman-child) is the agent of society.

Parenthetically, for this reason ("family" must be synonymous with children), the homosexual relationship cannot rationally be sanctioned by society as a "family"; there can never be a child of the "parties" (two men/two women). One of the parents will always be missing. Further, any child brought up in such a narrow and closed environment can never know a "family" (man/woman/child) as designed by nature or the essential qualities of a father (man) and a mother (woman). It is my belief, based on those cases involving homosexuals, that a child is embarrassed and psychologically scarred when it (the child) learns that one of its parents is homosexual. In every instance in which I had an opportunity to talk with a child of such a parent, in private, they said they were embarrassed when their friends learned, and that their relationship with that parent changed.

The individual family is the building block of a society, and is to a society what the cell is to the body or the second is to the minute. While each is a separate entity, the dependency of each on the other is such that they cannot be separated. It is impossible to analyze, look at, or write about, one, without touching the other.

Fromm explained:

> . . . the family. Freud has shown that the early experiences of the child have a decisive influence upon the formation of its character structure. If this is true, how then can we understand that the child, who—at least in our culture—has little contact with the life of society, is molded by it? The answer is not only that the parents—aside from certain individual variations—apply the educational patterns of the society they live in, but also that in their own personalities they represent the social character of their society or class. They transmit to the child what we may call the psychological atmosphere or the spirit of a society just by being as they are—namely representatives of this very spirit. The family thus may be considered to be the psychological agent of society (emphasis added).
>
> —*Escape from Freedom*, p. 167

The institution of marriage reflects the relationship between man and woman; the relationship between man and woman reflects the intellectual and emotional environment of the child; the emotional and intellectual environment of the child reflects the intellectual and emotional growth of the society. As children are taught, so the culture of which they are a part becomes. "As the twig is bent, so the tree inclines."

The annals of history clearly display man's resourcefulness in the invention of the plow, hoe, wheel, wagon, boat, ships, automobile, airplane, vehicles for space travel, medicines, telescopes and all the various other technologies that make life more pleasant and convenient.

So, what is the status of society today?

The pioneer movement (on earth) has ended. Mankind has, basically, conquered nature relative to physical comforts. Material conquest is no longer a valid goal. Mankind can now produce in abundance and variety what is sufficient not merely for subsistence but for luxury. We are now in the twenty-first century. Scientifically, there have been tremendous advances, some were predicted, some hoped for. We have placed men on the moon and brought them back. We can substitute human organs or make some artificial ones. The most distant points of our galaxy are, or will be, under our observation.

With all these achievements, Man should be feeling the greatest joy and satisfaction: living in the "Garden of Eden."

Tragically, this is not the case.

Today, society is in chaos: war, violence, starvation, hate, greed, envy, lust, drugs, homosexuality and all of the catalogue of crimes and vice—all of those events that fill the newspapers, magazines, periodicals, books and airways, and the people involved are from all age, gender, economic, social, ethnic and religious strata.

Judge Learned Hand has described it:

> A society in which each is willing to surrender only that for which he can see a personal equivalent is not a society at all; it is a group already in process of dissolution, and no one need concern himself to stay its inevitable end; it would be a hard choice between it and a totalitarian society. No Utopia, nothing but Bedlam, will automatically emerge from a regime of unbridled individualism, be it ever so rugged.
>
> —*The Practical Cogitator*, p. 322

Of what significance is there in going to the moon if one must return to an environment in which there is hate, discord, violence and hostility. In reality, man's technological achievements are hollow when viewed in light of his ability to appreciate them. Hollow because the scientific advances which man has achieved exceed his "psychological growth." Man, essentially, has built a picture gallery for the blind. It is as though man made great strides with half of himself and left the remaining half behind—as though only half of man's brain grew. Man's achievements for physical comfort and convenience are of little meaning until man can find "psychological comfort." Until man finds joy in life—in living—there can be no joy in any achievement or invention—only a temporary elation.

But this is not a situation that has **just happened.** The present is but a rehearsal of the past. Any period of recorded history will be a fair reflection of things as they are today.

I Sit and Look Out (1860)

I sit and look out upon all the sorrows of the world, and upon all
oppression and shame,
I hear secret convulsive sobs from young men at anguish with
themselves, remorseful after deeds done,

I see in low life the mother misused by her children, dying,
neglected, gaunt, desperate,
I see the wife misused by her husband, I see the treacherous
seducer of young women,
I mark the ranklings of jealousy and unrequited love attempted
to be hid, I see these sights on the earth,
I see the workings of battle, pestilence, tyranny, I see martyrs
and prisoners,
I observe a famine at sea, I observe the sailors casting lots who
shall be kill'd to preserve the lives of the rest,
I observe the slights and degradations cast by arrogant persons
upon laborers, the poor, and upon negroes, and the like;
All these—all the meanness and agony without end I sitting look
out upon,
See, hear, and am silent.

—Walt Whitman

Look at the annals. Rome, first century A. D., what did Juvenal tell us of the times, Satire I?

Vice

Say, when did Vice a richer harvest yield,
When did fell Avarice so engross the mind,
Or when the lust of play so curse mankind?

Money

O Gold, though Rome beholds no altars flame,
No temples rise to thy pernicious name,
Such as to Victory, Virtue, Faith are reared,

Or Concord, where the clamorous stork is heard;
Yet is thy divinity confessed,
Thy shrine established here in every breast.

Crimes

For virtue starves on Universal praise,
While crimes, in scorn of niggard Fate, afford
The ivory couches and the citron board,

The goblet high-embossed, the antique plate,
The lordly mansion, and the fair estate.
Nothing is left, nothing for future times
To add to the full catalogue of crimes.

The baffled sons must feel the same desires
And act the same mad follies as their sires.
Vice hath attained its zenith!

Sexual Promiscuity and Homosexuality

Oh, who can rest or taste the sweets of life
When sires debauch the son's too greedy wife,
When males to males, abjuring shame, are wed,
And beardless boys pollute the nuptial bed?

Why is our culture having the same problems of a culture two thousand years ago?

Hugo, in *Les Miserables*, p. 562, points out the reason:

> All history is only a long repetition. One century plagiarizes another.

The annals of history show little, if any, alteration in man's "psychological state" or in his relationship with Man.

Why has there been no growth?

Samuel Johnson explains:

> There are, indeed, many truths which time necessarily and certainly teaches, and which might, by those who have learned them by experience, be communicated to their successors at a cheaper rate: but dictates, though liberally enough bestowed, are generally without effect, the teacher gains few proselytes by instruction which his own behavior contradicts; and young men miss the benefit of counsel, because they are not very ready to believe that those who fell below them in practice, can much excel them in theory. Thus the progress of knowledge is retarded, the world is kept long in the same state, and every new race is to gain the prudence of their predecessors by committing and redressing the same miscarriages. *The Rambler*, No. 50, Saturday, 8 September 1750.

And where does one search to find the answer?

The answer to this question is, "the family (marriage)."

As the "family" goes, so goes the Nation—as set forth so succinctly by the Chinese proverb (paraphrased):

When the family is in chaos,
The community will be in chaos.
When the communities are in chaos,
The city will be in chaos.
When the cities are in chaos,
The Nation will be in chaos.

Aristotle made the same observation, as Bacon observed:

> Aristotle noteth well, that the nature of everything is best seen in his smallest portions, and for that cause **he inquireth the nature of a commonwealth, first in a family, and the simple conjugations of man and wife, parent and child, master and servant,**

> **which are in every cottage** (emphasis added): even so likewise the nature of this great city of the world and the policy thereof must be first sought in mean concordances and small portions. So we see how that secret of nature, of the turning of iron touched with the loadstone toward the north, was found out in needles of iron, not in bars of iron.

Historically, the "Institution of Marriage," generally speaking, has been treated by society with a calloused indifference, much as a "sacred cow," and there is very little regulation concerning the Institution of Marriage. Matrimony, the most hallowed of the social customs, has been a political "no, no" as to change. Unlike other aspects of the culture that have been inundated with innovation, marriage has, for all practical purposes, remained unchanged—even resistant to suggestions for change. Change has been suppressed by profound respect for inherited forms, especially by the concept of individualism.

The foundation of marriage has been, and continues to be, ignorance and immaturity. And, excluding the technicalities of incest, most anyone can get married and have children, without any real preconditions except age. Parties enter its portals without any understanding of the nature, design or essence of that being pursued. Consequently, the Institution of Marriage has been for centuries stagnant, like a pond into which no fresh water flows, heavy with putrification and decay.

In *The Future of Marriage in Western Civilization*, Edward Westermarck (New York, McMillan Company, 1936), begins the introduction:

> Recent years have been notable for an enormous literature dealing with sex and marriage. A dominate note of it is the assertion that the rapid changes in all human relationships which characterize our age are particularly great in the relationship between the sexes. Marriage is said to be facing a crisis: and some writers even speak of its collapse or "bankruptcy," and of "free love" taking its place.

> We are told marriage no longer binds, no longer unites; that "the new casual way of sexing has modified all our traditional thinking on the subject of holy matrimony": that the family has disintegrated beyond repair; that home has become merely "a place to dine and die; "that the time will come when marriage and the family have altogether ceased to exist."

And in Chapter 3, of the same work:

> Dr. Norman Haire writes: "Any moderately intelligent person who goes about the world with his eyes open—who is willing to face the truths of life even if they are disagreeable—must be struck by the appalling frequency of unhappiness in marriage. I can find no reason to believe that my circle of friends and acquaintances is an exceptional one, and if I am to judge by them I must conclude that a large majority of marriages are unsuccessful . . ."

Lederer and Jackson, some fifty years after *The Future Of Marriage in Western Civilization*, begin the introduction to their book, *The Mirages of Marriage*, (W. W. Norton & Company, Inc., New York, 1968):

> Year after year, in the United States, marriage has been discussed in public print, private session with undiminished confusion and increasing pessimism. Calamity always attracts attention, and in the United States, the state of marriage is a calamity. One-third of all marriages end in divorce within ten years, no one knows how many of the remaining two-thirds are calamitous. Recent surveys indicate that in affluent communities seven out of ten marriages fail.

The trend has continued.

Society is still influenced by the past; the male is still the favored sex, and still prone to wander; there are still expectations based on gender; there are still the same social differences, and marriage remains as it was under the common law, psychologically, even though the law has been modified, so to speak, to help protect the wife and child.

As in the past, the societal concept of marriage continues to be that matrimony is an honorable state, instituted by God for the continuation of the race and the mutual comfort of men and women.

There is in society an "understanding" that one can only find happiness and success—financially and socially—in marriage. In other words, the magic of ritual-marriage brings the well-being of the parties. Further, usually only married couples are invited to social events, single being odd. The act of marriage is expected to be the key to happiness as it represents an end rather than a beginning, a harbor rather than a journey.

Marriage is still, practically, available to all without regard to maturity, mentality or education. Marriage emancipates, and a "married couple" immediately enjoys, generally speaking, approval and privileges. As it is portrayed, the young and the discontented are lured to this, seeming, "harbor of bliss." As with the child's concept of the grown-up, only the assets are considered; there are no liabilities.

As marriage is portrayed, it (marriage) becomes, generally speaking, the fulfillment of a "dream" for the woman; for the man, it is the socially acceptable way for the male to gratify his sexual desire; it is a "refuge" from criticism, since it carries the implication of being a stable and responsible person; it is, also, a means of power, control, convenience and, more recently, another paycheck, which frees up for his personal use money that would otherwise have to be spent on the family.

For both, it represents a panacea.

To speak of marriage as an institution is a misnomer. An institution is something that serves to instruct—to enlighten. Being devoid of societal instruction, Marriage is an institution only in the sense that it is a necessary custom sanctioned and encouraged by society.

Marriage is so turbulent an institution that articles on how to patch up disintegrating marriages can be found in almost every issue of family magazines and daily newspapers. And mostly, the advice treats the symptoms . . . not the disease.

And in those marriages that survive, many will settle into a state in which mutual dependency may go hand in hand with mutual loathing, much like the pathological couple in *Who's Afraid of Virginia Woolf?*, by Edward Albee. Or have the pair come back, after a life of bickering, as cactus plants, a modern version of the myth of Philemon and Baucis.

In fact, those couples who remain together, generally speaking, find themselves in the paradoxical position of Byron's prisoner:

> My very chains and I grew friends, so much a long communion make us what we are.

As it is portrayed, "Marriage" is an "attractive nuisance" (in Law the doctrine involving the creation of that which attracts the very young and is dangerous because of their inability to perceive the peril). In fact, as it is represented, it is a CULTURAL BETRAYAL!

> To church in the morning, and there saw a wedding in the church, which I have not seen many a day; and the young people so merry **strange to see what delight we married people have to see those poor fools decoyed into our condition,** every man and woman gazing and smiling at them. Samuel Pepys: *Diary*, Dec. 25, 1665 (emphasis added)

While it was the search for the answers to the questions of "why and how" that brought about this work, the work as here presented was never envisioned; it evolved. It became, essentially, a study on the relationship between the family and all of the ills of society. But, in the process of evolving, the answers to the questions of "why and how" were found.

Where we are, is what this work is all about. Hopefully, it may give direction to where we can go. Since this study is "from effect to cause," it is necessary to show marriage (society) as it is, "to hold, as 'twere, the mirror up."

Matrimony—A Review

"No Social institution is more fateful for the human race than the home."

—*The Mature Mind*, Overstreet

The Institution of Marriage is the "stuff" that societies are made of.

So, how did it begin?

As always, to understand the phenomena, let's go to the beginning.

Procreation requires the man-woman relationship since mating (to cause to multiply) is biological; it is also pleasurable. Because it (mating—to cause to multiply) is pleasurable, social necessity required a way be found to fix responsibility for the care and maintenance of the product of this pleasure—the child—and the woman (vehicle for manufacturing the product of this pleasure) during the time the child was developing to be self-sufficient. So, the concept of "marriage" was devised. "Marriage," as instituted, was the ritual by which a man and a woman made known to their peers that they wanted to participate in the pleasure of mating. This desire to participate in the pleasure of mating was referred to as "love." When the man and woman made known to their peers their desire, there was a tacit understanding (an expectation from the peers) that they (man and woman, but primarily man) would be responsible for the care and maintenance of "the child" (the product of the pleasure), and the man would be responsible for the care and maintenance of the woman. The man was required to be responsible for the care and maintenance of the woman because it was believed that the woman did not have the capacity to take care of herself. Also, man had some knowledge (on faith) of where *he* had left *his* seed so that *he* could identify the persons to whom *he* wanted to leave *his* property at *his* death. So, the act of a man and woman living together in a union accepted by society began the societal concept of "Marriage." Having a wanderlust, Man (male of mankind), generally speaking, is ever present when there is opportunity for "making children," ever absent when there is opportunity for "raising children." He may drop his seed today and be gone tomorrow. After all, some things are more important than "raising children": war, golf, fishing, hunting, the "games," the "chase," the "tournaments," the "vineyards" or "the back forty," etc.

So, several myths were formulated:

1. "marriage" is a part of the "creation," ordained by God.
2. love (as it is conceived by society) conquers all, generally, and the expressed reason for getting married.
3. male superiority, dominus masculus.
4. union forever—even after death. "What God has joined together, let no man put asunder."
5. mother's love.

These myths are an integral part of marriage, and have been nurtured and taught generation after generation by the "silent forces" and the "thought forces." That which is taught by these means are, essentially, the concepts or beliefs that are accepted as "truths" in a given culture or society and transmitted by parents, members of society, schools and organized religions. These "forces" are classified by sociology as mores and customs. These "forces" teach, mold, develop and control cultures as to the do's and don'ts of behavior, and societal punishments for violation. Mores and customs are fed repeatedly in bits and pieces directly and subtly, though purposefully, through various means—literature, casual conversations, looks, songs, games, approval, disapproval, criticism, etc.—to people from the day they are born until they die, and are as "bands of iron."

The myths of marriage have been so romanticized as a "reality" by religion, fairy tales, folklore, poetry, stories, novels, movies, advertising, television, etc. that they have, in fact, become a reality for most people.

There is a tacit understanding in society that it is a "No, No" to remain single:

> They [the unmarried] dream away their time without friendship, without fondness and are driven to rid themselves of the day, for which they have no use, by childish amusements or vicious delights. They act as beings under the constant sense of some known inferiority, that fills their minds with rancor and their tongues with censure. They are peevish at home and malevolent abroad; and, as the outlaws of human nature, make it their business and their pleasure to disturb that society which debars them from its privileges.
>
> —Samuel Johnson: *Rasselas XXVI*, Penguin Books, 1976

The societal concept of marriage is the husband provides the living and the wife takes care of the home and "raises the husband's children"; thus was born the myth of "mother's love."

These beliefs were a part of common law.

> For man, marriage is regarded as a station; for women, as a vocation. "Women and Marriage"
>
> —*Concerning Women*, Suzanne LaFollette

For the woman, marriage is, still, the fulfillment of a "dream," a necessity for identity and security, as stated succinctly by Elinor Glyn:

> Marriage is the aim and end of all sensible girls, because it is the meaning of life.

And Jane Porter:

In the career of female fame, there are few prizes to be obtained which can vie with the obscure state of a beloved wife or a happy mother.

Moliere:

A husband is a plaster that cures all ills of girlhood.

Marriage—The Illusory

"As the glow of Love's inward fire increases, so the frenzy of the lover's suit."

—Gottfried

Practically, "marriage" must be viewed from the aspect of the "avowal of love," as this is the umbrella under which the union begins.

"Romantic love"—ahhhhhh . . . ! all have heard of it—is the experience of feeling a "oneness" with another without any foundation. It happens when a man and woman, who are attracted to each other, let the "wall of strangers" break down; that is, they tell each other their secret thoughts and feelings.

What is the common process of marriage? Johnson states it well (there has been little change):

> A youth and maiden, meeting by chance, are brought together by artifice, exchange glances, reciprocate civilities, go home and dream of one another. Having little to divert attention, or diversify a thought, they find themselves uneasy when they are apart, and therefore conclude that they shall be happy together.
>
> —*Rasselas*, XXIX.

(Postscript: and more recently, begin having sex.)

Emerson, in his essay *Love*, describes it this way:

> Little think the youth and maiden who are glancing at each other across crowded rooms, with eyes so full of mutual intelligence,—of the precious fruit long hereafter to proceed from this new, quiet external stimulus.

From exchanging glances, they advance to acts of courtesy, of gallantry, then to fiery passion, to plighting troth and marriage. Passion beholds its object as a perfect unit. The soul is wholly embodied, and the body is wholly ensouled.

"Her pure and eloquent blood
Spoke in her cheeks, and so distinctly wrought,
That one might almost say her body thought."
Life, with this pair, has no other aim, asks no more than
Juliet—than Romeo."

The lovers delight in endearments, in avowals of love, in comparisons of their regards. When alone, they solace themselves with the remembered image of the other. Does that other see the same star, the same melting cloud, read the same book, feel the same emotion that now delight me? They try and weigh their affection, and adding up all costly advantages, friends, opportunities, properties, exult in discovering that willingly, joyfully, they would give all as a ransom for the beautiful, the beloved head, not one hair of which shall be harmed.

Balzac observed:

Two beings on the eve of joining always deceive each other; but the deception is innocent and involuntary. Each, of course, stands in the best light; they are rivals as to which makes the most promising show, and at that time form a favorable idea of themselves which they cannot afterwards come up to.

It is a "promising show."

This intimacy brings an illusion of closeness, of oneness; it is an exhilarating and exciting experience! They "fall in love"; it is "love at first sight." How sweet it is . . .

It is an international phenomenon . . . timeless . . .

Listen . . . from China . . . over 2000 years ago. . .

In Praise of a Maiden

Oh! the maiden, so handsome and coy,
For a pledge gave a slim rosy reed.
Than the reed is she brighter, my joy;
    On her loveliness how my thoughts feed!

In the pastures a t'e blade she sought,
    And she gave it, so elegant, rare.
Oh! the grass does not dwell in my thought,
    But the donor, more elegant, fair.

A Love-Song

The moon comes forth, a splendid sight;
More winning far that lady bright,
    Object of my desire!
Deep-seated is my anxious grief;
In vain I seek to find relief,
    While glows the secret fire.

The rising moon shines mild and fair;
More bright is she, whose beauty rare
    My heart with longing fills.
With eager wish I pine in vain;
O for relief from constant pain,
    Which through my bosom thrills!

The Lament of a Lover

All round the marsh's shores are seen

Valerian flowers and rushes green
But lovelier is that Beauty rare,
Handsome and large, and tall and fair.
I wish and long to call her mine,
Doomed with the longing still to pine.
Nor day nor night e'er brings relief;
My inmost heart is full of grief.

Around the marsh, in rich display,
Grow rush and lotus flowers, all gay.
But not with her do they compare,
So tall and large, majestic, fair.
Both day and night, I nothing speed;
Still clings to me the aching need.
On side, on back, on face, I lie,
But vain each change of posture try.

From France . . . Abelard . . . Abelard was thirty-eight, Heloise eighteen and the year 1118 A.D. "There was in Paris a young girl named Heloise, the niece of a canon, Fulbert, . . ." we read in the rueful autobiographical letter known as Abelard's *Historia Calamitatum*:

> I had hitherto lived continently, but now was casting my eyes about, and I saw that she possessed every attraction that lovers seek; nor did I regard my success as doubtful, when I considered my fame and my godly person, and also her love of letters. Inflamed with love, I thought how I could best become intimate with her. It occurred to me to obtain lodgings with her uncle, on the plea that household cares distracted me from study. Friends quickly brought this about, the old man being miserly and yet desirous of instruction for his niece. He eagerly entrusted her to my tutorship, and begged me to give her all the time I could take from my lectures, authorizing me to see her at any hour of the day or night and punish her when necessary. I marveled with what simplicity he

confided a tender lamb to a hungry wolf. . . . Well, what need to say more: we were united first by the one roof above us, and then by our hearts.

From Italy . . .

When I saw thee for the first time, it seemed to me that paradise was opened, and that the angels were coming, one by one, all to rest on thy lovely face, all to rest on thy beautiful head; thou bindest me in chains, and I cannot loose myself.

—J. Casell "chants popul de l'Itali, 21"

From England . . .

There is a Lady Sweet and Kind

There is a lady sweet and kind,
Was never face so pleased my mind;
I did but see her passing by,
And yet I love her till I die.

Her gesture, motion, and her smiles,
Her wit, her voice, my heart beguiles,
Beguiles my heart, I know not why,
And yet I love her till I die. . . .

Cupid is winged and doth range,
Her country so my love doth change:
But change she earth, or change she sky,
Yet will I love her till I die.

—Anonymous

The Passionate Shepherd to His Love

Come live with me and be my Love,
And we will all the pleasures prove
That hills and valleys, dales and fields,
Or woods or steeply mountain yields.

And we will sit upon the rocks,
And see the shepherds feed their flocks
By shallow rivers, to whose falls
Melodious birds sing madrigals.

And I will make thee beds of roses
And a thousand fragrant posies;
A cap of flowers, and a kirtle
Embroidered all with leaves of myrtle;

A gown made of the finest wool
Which from our pretty lambs we pull;
Fair-lined slippers for the cold,
With buckles of the purest gold;

A belt of straw and ivy buds
With coral clasps and amber studs—
And if these pleasures may thee move,
Come live with me and by my Love.

The shepherd swains shall dance and sing
For thy delight each May morning—
If these delights thy mind may move,
Then live with me and by my Love.

—Christopher Marlowe

And, so, with wistful eyes that meet, groping hands that clasp, lips that call to ears that hear, they join as husband and wife.

A more practical description of this event would be this:

Woman, having found love (security), man, convenience (sex, cook, maid), they marry (or live together), and then, strong in their relationship, begin pursuit of the realities of life (wealth, power, fame), with children being evidence to the world of a very close relationship (eat your heart out world), or negligence (we really wanted eight), knowing "what God (magistrate, Probate Judge, Notary Public) hath put together, no man (lawyer not included) can put asunder." And on this foundation, it all begins.

And, now we hear . . .

The Rejoicings of a Bridegroom

With axle creaking, all on fire I went,
To fetch my young and lovely bride.
No thirst or hunger pangs my bosom rent—
    I only longed to have her by my side.
I feast with her, whose virtue fame had told,
Nor need we friends our rapture to behold.

The long-tailed pheasants surest covert find,
    Amid the forest on the plain.
Here from my virtuous bride, of noble mind,
    And person tall, I wisdom gain.
I praise her while we feast, and to her say,
"The love I bear you ne'er will know decay."

“Poor we may be; spirits and viands fine
        My humble means will not afford.
But what we have, we’ll taste and not repine;
        From us will come no grumbling word.
And though to you virtue I can add,
Yet we will sing and dance, in spirit glad.”

“I oft ascend that lofty ridge with toil,
        And hew large branches from the oaks;
Then of their leafy glory them I spoil,
        And fagots from with vigorous strokes.
Returning tired, your matchless grace I see,
And my whole soul dissolves in ecstasy."

“To the high hills I looked, and urged each steed;
        The great road next was smooth and plain.
Up hill, o’er dale, I never slackened speed;
        Like lute-string sounded every rein.
I knew, my journey ended, I should come
To you, sweet bride, the comfort of my home.”

We have heard from the Bridegroom, so . . . what does the bride have to say?

Enough! she cries, henceforth thou art
The friend and master of my heart.
No other covenant I require
Than this: “I take thee for my wife.”
That done, enjoy thy heart’s desire,
Of me and mine, the Lord for life.

—*Raynouard Lexique Roman*, 1.139, Roman de Faufre

To whom thus Eve with *perfect beauty* adorn’d.
Author and Disposer, what thou bidst

Unargued I obey; So God ordains;
God is thy law, *thou mine*: to know no more.
—*Paradise Lost,* IV.634–38, Milton.

The dream for the marriage is excited by a relationship that does not exist. The marriage, generally speaking, is begun with short-term planning; each enters into the union for the purpose of achieving or fulfilling some felt personal immediate need or goal which is expected to be accomplished through the union with the other. They are content with the ardor of desire. Alien to themselves, alien to each other, blinded by desire, they bind themselves to one another for a lifetime journey "o'er unknown seas, to unknown lands," believing they have found the bluebird of happiness. Thus, the marriage begins with the relationship on an "illusory high."

From the poem "Cinderella" in *Transformations*, by Anne Sexton:

Cinderella and the prince
lived, they say, happily ever after,
like two dolls in a museum case
never bothered by diapers or dust . . .

It is generally assumed that in a "Marriage" (the act of joining as man and wife), the parties to that Marriage have a close, personal relationship, even by the parties. But, the panacea that is envisioned by most parties for a marriage presumes a relationship that does not exist. The attraction that each feels for the other is not based on a consideration of intelligence, temperaments, habits, tastes, etc., and is, therefore, irrational. Being irrational, it is an illusion; that is, each sees in the other qualities of character that do not exist. Essentially, the relationship is a mirage—as defined: anything that appears to be real but is not.

Marriage—The Reality

> "When billing and cooing results in matrimony, the billing always comes after the cooing."
>
> —Tom Masson

The term "marriage" undergoes a metamorphosis: first, to signify the act or ceremony by which a man and woman are joined in wedlock, and then, after the ceremony, to denote their civil status with the attendant rites and duties imposed by law. So, too, does the relationship between the parties after the ceremony.

> The union (the marriage) which is thus effected, and which adds a new value to every atom in nature, for it transmutes every thread throughout the whole web of relation into a golden ray, and bathes the soul in a new and sweeter element, **is yet a temporary state.** (emphasis added)
>
> —*Love*, Emerson essay.

Marriage, The Reality, is an effort to portray a marriage from the beginning to the end. It is impossible to portray the actual event of the disintegration of a marriage. The actual event is subtle, and time consuming, as water running over rock—an imperceptible erosion. One can only give a few highlights. Even the parties, when questioned, can remember little more than a few highlights, since there is much suppression and rationalization, with feelings of guilt and fear.

Any relationship can only be as lasting as the foundation on which it is formed. In the initial euphoric state, there were no thoughts of duties and responsibilities or the significance of the act.

Marriage, the reality, is an after-the-ceremony occurrence—a realization of the magnitude of marriage. It is much like waking up with a "hang-over" after a night of revelry, although more subtle.

Eric Hodgins, in *Episode*, noted such:

> There's post-operative depression, post-partum depression, post-graduate depression and post-marital depression.

In the finding and providing for the furnishing of the living accommodations, planning meals, buying groceries, cooking and cleaning, arranging credit for various purchases, going to and coming from work, visiting and entertaining family and friends, sickness, buying clothes, paying bills, making decisions on priorities, choosing and selecting in an infinite number of ways, the husband and wife, essentially, experience the activities that are the realities of living for the first time. In the beginning, as with all new experiences, generally speaking, it was fun and exciting. In these activities, in time, the husband and wife find there are differences of opinion and arguing ensues. In the activities of living, they begin to know and learn each other in depth. Reality destroys the illusions, and brings forth, gradually, more differences of opinion and arguing. These activities, too, gradually, reveal the aspects of the other to each that were subconsciously overlooked, rationalized or concealed; in essence, each, gradually, learns and discovers the real person of the other—personality, maturity, disposition, intellectual capacity, character traits.

> The soul which is in the soul of each, craving for a perfect beatitude, detects incongruities, defects, and disproportion in the behavior of the other. Hence arises surprise, expostulation, and pain.
>
> —*Love*, Emerson essay.

As the evaporation of a heavy fog gradually reveals the landscape, time dispels the illusions of marriage (a panacea, a port); and the illusions of love (a oneness, togetherness, love conquers all) and leaves the parties naked in their relationship.

The parties have eaten from the tree of knowledge; they are no longer in the "Garden of Eden"; all illusions have been dispelled.

As the luster of passion fades, as intimacy cools excitement, the attitude of the husband changes:

> Now, love in young men is not love but lust, and, as its ultimate end is pleasure, it ceases once that subject has been attained; and what appeared to be love must disappear because it cannot pass the limits assigned to it by nature, whereas true affection knows none of such limitations. I mean to say that no sooner had Don Fernando enjoyed the farmer's daughter than his desires weakened and his amorous impulses cooled. If at first he had pretended that he would absent himself in order to get rid of his passions, he now earnestly endeavored to go away to avoid fulfilling his promises.
>
> —*Don Quixote*, Cervantes

The husband does not feel the same relatedness (oneness) to the wife as the wife toward him; for the husband, there is no fusion of identity with the wife as there is for the wife with the husband. The husband's concept of oneness is the same as "possession." In fact, the husband's attitude toward his wife has strong similarities with his attitude toward his dog: in both relationships, he takes pride in looks, performance and obedience; in both relationships he believes he can take whatever liberties he desires; in both relationships he expects to be "master." "Love," for the husband is totally related to "power" and "convenience." The husband develops a dichotomous attitude toward the marriage. He enjoys his role as head of the family (power) and the convenience (satisfaction of the senses, i.e. sex, food, clothes washed and cleaned, etc.), but the responsibilities of marriage remain and they chafe! The husband is annoyed by the restriction and responsibilities of marriage; he feels trapped. He is resentful. The husband gradually changes from focusing his attention on the wife and the home to his job, hobbies, friends and, many, drinking (all of which are socially acceptable). Soon the home becomes, for the man, a retreat from his job, outside activities and hobbies—a place of convenience, comfort and sustenance—a traditional cultural symbol.

The wife, who becomes more isolated, feels the change in the attitude of the husband toward her, and there will be vocal expressions of such by her to him. Of course, there will be denials by the husband, but, many times, there will be temporary changes of behavior. More and more, the wife finds that she is doing most of the tasks at the home alone and is seeing less and less of the husband. This leaves the wife distant in their relationship.

> It's as hard to get a man to stay home after you've married him as it was to get him to go home before you married him.
>
> —Helen Rowland

So, how do they recover a relationship that has grown cold?

A child, of course.

Upon receiving the news, the husband, initially, showed joy, joy, joy—a cultural tradition; the joy, in time, fades as did his passion for the wife.

After the arrival of the child, the life style changes.

The wife no longer feels as alone, and the parties now have a toy, a plaything, a possession, a display, an exhibit, a spectacle, an exhibition and a show piece. Also, it is evidence to the wife that her husband loves her.

The excitement of the arrival of the child is soon cooled by the needs and temperament of the child. The child must be cared for: fed, clothed, bathed, and it has a habit of making a lot of noise at various hours. Taking care of the child, generally speaking, will become the wife's responsibility. The husband feels squeezed, financially, when food, clothes, diapers, medicine and various other items must be bought for the child. Within a short time, the child becomes a two-edged sword, pleasure and responsibility, but more a sense of responsibility than pleasure, especially for the wife.

The husband's attitude of cooperation gradually fades, and, again, the wife finds that she is doing most of the tasks alone, and is seeing less and less of the husband.

The husband is aware of the expectations of society: he is to provide a living for the family; the wife is to take care of the home and children. And "minimal" becomes his response to the marriage: minimal amount of "his" money and minimal amount of "his" time. Everything (time and money) above "minimal" is his to do with as he pleases; and, at times, things like rent, utilities, food, clothes, etc. must take second place to his "wants." Further, he believes that he is entitled to the earnings of the wife. And herein arises one of the thorns of the marriage: the wife believes that his "time," his "earnings," her "time," her "earnings" belong to the family.

In the cultural tradition, "avoid" and "delegate" become the husband's watchwords: avoid home and delegate to the wife all of the responsibilities of the home and marriage. The wife is expected to work, stay at home when she is not working, keep house, cook, attend to the children, be available for sex at his pleasure, pay the bills from her paycheck, allow him total freedom and the use of his money for his individual pleasure.

The wife and child experience firsthand the observation made by Judge Caldwell:

> The rule is without exception that whenever the exclusive power of making or administering the law (home) is committed for any extended period to a single man (husband) or a few men—to a caste—the progressive restriction of the liberty of the people (wife and children) follow.

A sense of divisiveness comes into the relationship, although the wife takes on the delegated responsibilities. Male domination arrives! Though resentful, the wife accepts the roles of mother, maid and mistress to the husband to appease, and for harmony in the home for the children. The marriage settles into the rut of conventionality. This means husband does what he wishes and wife does what husband wishes.

The parties begin the pursuit of different interests: the man—politics, sports, hunting, fishing, fraternal organizations, etc.; the woman—cooking, sewing, church activities, home and children, etc. In effect, the husband and wife almost live separate lives, with minimal contact.

After the personal relationship between the man and woman has totally deteriorated, another illusion is born: "the marital relationship." Now, everything (work, household chores, paying bills, social activities, etc.) is done under the auspices of "the marital relationship"—duty. Even though "love" is expressed by each for the other, it is the facade of the relationship for the role of marriage.

> When I look back, the Garden is a dream to me. It was beautiful, surpassingly beautiful, enchantingly beautiful; and now it is lost, and I shall not see it any more.
>
> The Garden is lost, but I have found him, and am content. He loves me as well as he can; I love him with all the strength of my passionate nature, and this, I think, is proper to my youth and sex. If I ask myself why I love him, I find I do not know, and do not really much care to know; so I suppose that this kind of love is not a product of reasoning and statistics, like one's love for other reptiles and animals. I think that this must be so. I love certain birds because of their song; but I do not love Adam on account of his singing—no, it is not that; the more he sings, the more I do not get reconciled to it. Yet I ask him to sing, because I wish to learn to like everything he is interested in. I am sure I can learn because at first I could not stand it; but now I can. It sours the milk, but it doesn't matter; I can get used to that kind of milk.

It is not on account of his brightness that I love him—no, it is not that. He is not to blame for his brightness, such as it is, for he did not make it himself; he is as God made him, and that is sufficient. There was a wise purpose in it, that I know. In time it will develop, though I think it will not be sudden; and besides, there is no hurry; he is well enough just as he is.

It is not on account of his gracious and considerate ways and his delicacy that I love him. No, he has lacks in these regards, but he is well enough just so, and is improving.

It is not on account of his industry that I love him—no, it is not that. I think he has it in him, and I do not know why he conceals it from me. It is my only pain. Otherwise he is frank and open with me, now. I am sure he keeps nothing from me but this. It grieves me that he should have a secret from me, and sometimes it spoils my sleep, thinking of it, but I will put it out of my mind; it shall not trouble my happiness, which is otherwise full to overflowing.

It is not on account of his education that I love him—no, it is not that. He is self-educated, and does really know a multitude of things, but they are not so.

It is not on account of his chivalry that I love him—no, it is not that. He told on me, but I do not blame him; it is a peculiarity of sex, I think, and he did not make his sex. Of course I would not have told on him, I would have perished first; but that is a peculiarity of sex, too, and I do not take credit for it, for I did not make my sex.

Then why is it that I love him? Merely because he is masculine, I think.

At bottom he is good, and I love him for that, but I could love him without it. If he should beat me and abuse me, I should go on loving him. I know it. It is a matter of sex, I think.

He is strong and handsome, and I love him for that, and I admire him and am proud of him, but I could love him without those qualities. If he were plain, I should love him; if he were a wreck, I should love him; and I would work for him, and slave over him, and pray for him, and watch by his bedside until I died.

Yes, I think I love him merely because he is mine and masculine. There is no other reason, I suppose. And so I think it is as I first said: that this kind of love is not a product of reasonings and statistics. It just comes—none knows whence—and cannot explain itself. And doesn't need to.

It is what I think. But I am only a girl, and the first that has examined this matter, and it may turn out that in my ignorance and inexperience I have not got it right.

—"The Diary of Adam and Eve," Mark Twain.

Sex, for the wife, is not passion but an obligation. The "thrill" of the marriage is found in the "new": clothes, cars, home, furnishings, etc. The family is "doing things together" when they are watching the man's television programs, eating at a fast-food restaurant and taking an occasional outing or vacation.

In conformity with custom, so long as the husband continues to tell the wife that he loves her, she continues her role of mother, maid and mistress. Essentially, the marriage is held together by the tenuous bond of "marriage." It is, simply, a living arrangement; a duality without synthesis. The wife is managing the husband's household.

Maggie. Marriage is a business of taking care of a man and rearing his children. . . . It ain't meant to be no perpetual honeymoon.

—*The Women*, Act I, Clare Boothe Luce, 1936.

The woman learns the truth of Byron's observation that "love, to the man's life, is a thing apart. . . ." The woman feels the marriage vows were, effectively, a coronation ceremony for the man and sacrificial rites for her.

The attitude of cooperation gradually fades.

Ultimately, there are numerous quarrels and unpleasant skirmishes, usually over money and usually in front of the children. The result is status struggle (the king will not be dethroned), and bitter competitiveness (the family needs will be provided in spite of husband's "wants"). The conflict between man's "wants" and family "needs" continue.

The new generation is this culture's best barometer registering its social unrest, its conflicts, and its impact on the individual psyche. The many lives that follow are a psychoanalyst's look at our young men and women; at who and what they are, what they feel, and what they strive for, and what pressures move them and us. The collective thrust of their lives point toward one overwhelming fact: this culture is at war and young people are in the front lines.

—*The Age of Sensation*, Herbert Hindin, 1975

The woman's only weapons to achieve the family's needs and to maintain a semblance of self-respect and identity are her tongue (nagging) and her body (sex); both are socially acceptable. The man has a much greater variety in his arsenal.

1. physical abuse—bones broken, cuts, bruises, miscarriages from violence, twisted arms, teeth knocked out, busted lips, all needing medical treatment.
2. personal degradation.
3. verbal abuse—"you slut, whore, ignoramus, dumb bitch, silly ass, mean, vicious."
4. emotional uncertainty—constantly leaving and returning, threatening to leave, husband participating in open and admitted adulterous relationship.
5. threats of physical abuse.
6. slavery—wife doing all housework, washing, cooking, taking care of children and working at outside job.
7. servitude—husband takes her wages and gives her what he wants her to have.
8. embarrassment and humiliation—open flirting by husband, put down in front of others, criticism of sexual conduct, constant drinking and failing to provide necessities, requiring an accounting of where she's been upon returning home from an errand.
9. neglect—refusal to buy clothes, provide medical treat-

ment, leaving her at home while he goes constantly, prohibiting her from going anyplace including her family, refusing to take her anyplace.

10. aloneness—the feeling that she must bear most responsibilities (financial, discipline of children, decisions of household, etc.) by herself.

> God has given the man greater wit, better strength, better courage, to compel the woman to obey by reason or force; and to the woman beauty, fair countenance, sweet words, to make the man obey her again for love. Thus each obeyeth and commandeth the other; and they two together rule the house so long as they remain in one.
>
> —Sir Thomas Smith

The "nagging" by the wife, in reality, is a plead—asking the husband to be the man he was in the **courting relationship**, and to accept a shared responsibility for the marriage.

Even though she realizes she is an object for his use after his desire has cooled and her illusion of togetherness and a common goal has been dispelled, she is still willing to go more than 50–50. For her, the marriage is a commitment; she struggles to keep it intact. She rationalizes that all marriages have "their ups and downs."

Over and over and over again, the wife tries to talk with the husband about the marriage—to no avail. His feelings are that the wife is just "blaming" him, that she wants him to be "perfect," or that he "just cannot talk to her." Everything is fine as far as he is concerned; he cannot understand her discontent.

The wife learns of the husband:

> Immodest creature, you do not want a woman who will accept your faults, you want one who pretends that you are faultless—one who will caress the hand that strikes her and kiss the lips that lie to her.
>
> —*Intimate Journal*, Susan B. Anthony, (1834) 1926

Nor does she get any consolation, after she has overcome her embarrassment to speak of it, from family or friends:

"Men are that way."
"Pamper him."
"You've made your bed, now lie in it."
"You took him for better or worse."
"Hang in there."
"It'll get better."
"What God hath joined, let no man put asunder."

From these encounters with society, the wife learns that, in the arena of marriage, the rules and concepts totally favor the man—psychologically and practically.

As time goes by, when the wife tries to talk about the marriage, the husband begins to tell her, in front of the children, that she can leave the home anytime, and he would be glad if she did.

> Thus, for example, a man may treat his wife very sadistically and tell her repeatedly that she can leave the house any day and that he would be only too glad if she did. . . . But if she musters up enough courage to declare that she will leave him, something quite unexpected to both of them may happen; he will become desperate, break down, and beg her not to leave him; he will say he cannot live without her, and will declare how much he loves her and so on. Usually, being afraid of asserting herself anyhow, she will be prone to believe him, change her decision and stay. At this point the play starts again. He resumes his old behavior, she finds it increasingly difficult to stay with him, explodes again, he breaks down again, she stays, and so on and on many times. There are thousands upon thousands of marriages . . . in which this cycle is repeated again and again, and the magic circle is never broken through.
>
> —*Escape from Freedom*, Fromm, pg. 167

The union continues: frequency becomes habit, habit license, license necessity, necessity, the marriage. She clings to the hope that he will soon be the way he used to be.

But, such is not to be.

> "All who marry for love either beat their wives or run away from them."
>
> —*Disraeli*, Act I, Louis N. Parker (1911)

Don Jose and the Donna Inez led
For sometime an unhappy sort of life,
Wishing each other not divorced but dead;
They lived respectably as man and wife,
Their conduct was exceedingly well bred,
And gave no outward sign of inward strife,
Until at length the smothered fire broke out,
And put the business past all kind of doubt.

—Lord Byron

Reflections on Marriage

Some recent material about marriage—motivated by the increase in divorce—seems to imply that the institution of marriage has only recently "fallen from grace." This is not the case.

It is reputed that the philosopher Thales, who was included among the seven wise men of the ancient world, made answer to the question: when should a man marry?

> A young man not yet, an elder man not at all.

Montaigne made this observation:

> The land of marriage has this peculiarity, that strangers are desirous of inhabiting it, whilst its natural inhabitants would willingly be banished from thence.

Lord Byron, while writing *Don Juan*, had not decided "whether to make him [Don Juan] end in hell or end in an unhappy marriage, not knowing which would be the severest." In *Rasselas*, Princess Nekayah did not know "whether marriage be more than one of the innumerable modes of human misery." Even in Luggnagg, a land of Gulliver's travels, a marriage between "struddlebergs" (immortals—identified by a red circular spot on the forehead which was a sign they should never die) was dissolved as a matter of course by the courtesy of the kingdom as soon as the younger of the two came to be four score:

> For the law thinks it a reasonable indulgence, that those who are

condemned without any fault of their own, should not have their misery doubled by the load of a wife.

Emerson thought marriage a trap with some compensating factors, "as if she [the minding mother] felt that she owed us some indemnity . . . "

Walt Whitman:

Let marriage slip down among fools and be for none but fools! *Respondez*!

Harriet Martineau opined:

The older I have grown, the more serious and irremediable have seemed to me the evils and disadvantages of married life as it exists among us at this time.

—"Women," *Society in America*, Vol. III page 1837

. . . when a woman marries, it may in general be understood that she makes choice of the management of a household, and the bringing up of a family, as the first call upon her exertions, during as many years of her life as may be required for the purpose; and that she renounces, not all other objects and occupations, but all which are not consistent with the requirements of this.

—*The Subjection of Women*, p. 295, John Mills

Emma Goldman felt:

Marriage is primarily an economic arrangement, an insurance pact . . . Its returns are insignificantly small compared with the investments. In taking out an insurance policy one pays for it in dollars and cents, always at liberty to discontinue the payments. If, however, woman's premium is a husband, she pays for it with her name, her privacy, her self-respect, her very life, "until death doth part." . . . Man, too, pays his toll.

—"Marriage and Love," *Anarchism and Other Essays.*

One must wonder, as Johnson:

> What can be expected but disappointment and repentance from choice made in the immaturity of youth, and the ardor of desire, without judgment, without foresight, without an inquiry after conformity of opinions, similarity of manners, rectitude of judgment, or purity of sentiment?

Of course there are those marriages that are knowingly contracted out of necessity, for revenge, on the rebound, to escape, for a front, to achieve wealth, for social status, to reform the other, out of spite, a "home," or any one of a myriad of reasons, albeit the stated reason is for "love."

The Autopsy

> "They stood before the altar and supplied the fires themselves in which their fat was fried."
>
> —Ambrose Bierce

Why do many husbands abuse their wives and children?

Why do wives, with children in most cases, continue in a relationship in which they (and children in many cases) are abused by their husbands?

And what is the "support system" by which marriages continue to function when all vital aspects of a meaningful relationship are dead?

Why are most divorces filed by the wives?

Why do most husbands prefer the ground of "physical cruelty" in an action for a divorce against them by their wives?

Essentially, why do most marriages fail?

It was the search for the answers to these questions that brought this work about. And, strangely, the answers to all of these questions are found in a statement of Thomas Wolfe:

> We are the sum of all the moments of our lives—all that is ours is in them: we cannot escape it or conceal it. Each of us is all the sums he has not counted.
>
> —*Look Homeward Angel*

". . . the sum of all the moments of our lives . . ." includes all the myths, fairy tales, customs, mores and religious dogmas concerning the aspects of the male and female and love and marriage which have been taught, practiced and sanctioned by cultures in which one lives, and in which the relationship for a "marriage" is formed, from the first meeting of the parties to the ceremony. It also includes all that is **NOT TAUGHT**.

In the Western culture, the customs and mores for "marriage" are a "mixture." Looking at the mixture, the reasons why marriage has not been well received becomes obvious, and the questions that began the search are answered.

The mixture—societal apathy, passions, social urges, ignorance, contrary purposes, and religious dogma—makes the institution of marriage something of a mythical concept. A myth, as the word is usually defined:

> One of the fictions or half-truths forming part of the ideology of a society; a notion based more on tradition or convenience than on fact.

Societal Urges and Apathy

While society has failed to give to the institution of marriage a foundation, structure, or stated function, it urges marriage with the inference that one can only find happiness and success—financially and socially—in marriage. And a married couple immediately enjoy approval and privileges. Yet, there are few regulations concerning mentality or maturity, or requiring instructions on the selection of a mate, economics of the home, or the bearing, rearing and education of children or responsibility to society. Nor have the parties been made aware of the intricacies of the involvement, or the mandatory personal adjustments that must be made. There is the inference that no preparations and no adjustments are necessary for marriage. So, the young and discontented are lured to this harbor of bliss. Essentially, society has been content for "marriage" to be boy and girl meet, fall in love, marry, and live happily ever after, and it has continued without guidance much like a runaway horse.

The institution of marriage has, generally, served only to satisfy the physical needs of the parties, with the union being maintained by the impetus of sex, accumulating material wealth, raising children and coercion (fear, the law, and religious dogma). Sharing, for the parties, has been, generally, on very limited basis—i.e., vacations, eating out, going to movies.

Whether apathy or ignorance, society has failed to recognize that it is the relationship between the husband and wife that makes a marriage, and not the vows. This attitude is clearly shown in a Court opinion concerning marriage:

> It is generally recognized that the public policy relating to mar-

> riage is to foster and protect it, to make it a permanent and public institution, to encourage the parties to live together, and to prevent separation. This policy finds expression in probably every state in this country in legislative enactments designed to prevent the sundering of the marriage ties for slight and trivial causes, or in any case except on a full and satisfactory proof of such facts as the legislature has declared to be cause for divorce. Such provisions find their justification only in this well organized interest of the state in the permanency of the marriage relation. Other contracts may be modified, restricted, or enlarged, or entirely released upon the consent of the parties. Not so with marriage. The relation once formed, the law steps in and holds the parties to various obligations and liabilities. It is an institution, in the maintenance of which in its purity the public is deeply interested, for it is the foundation of the family and of society, without which there would be neither civilization nor progress.
>
> —*Brown v. Brown,* 56 S.E.2d 330, 333.

This flaw was noted, too, by Suzanne LaFollette:

> Where divorce is allowed at all . . . society demands a specific grievance of one party against the other . . . The fact that marriage may be a failure spiritually is seldom taken into account.
>
> —*The Beginnings of Emancipation, Concerning Women*, p. 1926.

Within the societal view of marriage, there is inconsistency and contradiction. While society on the one hand encourages marriage and holds the parties to the "contract," on the other hand, there are no requirements that mandate instructions on the complexities of marriage. The contradictions in society define the degree of enlightenment:

1. Society reveres marriage and denounces divorce but fails to regulate or define the scope and purpose of marriage.

2. Society teaches antagonism between the sexes (male superiority), and expects cooperation in marriage.
3. Society reveres marriage and denounces divorce but fails to give instruction to the parties of the aspects and involvement of marriage and expects success in the marriage.
4. Society adores children and denounces abortion but fails to insure the environment in which the child will be exposed will be safe and will encourage the proper physical and psychological development.
5. Society continually denounces violence but does nothing to prevent it in the home.

Consequently, women and children have been, and are, sacrificial lambs on the altar of the Institution of Marriage, since it is, generally speaking, their physical and mental well-being that is most affected.

Therefore, the institution of marriage has been the seed of rot for society—the soil that nourished the growth of violence, hate, ignorance, war, selfishness, dependency, anxiety, frustration, and has been a gross impediment to enlightenment.

Passions

In folly ripe, in reason rotten.

When a man and woman are attracted to each other, generally speaking, it is by perceived physical beauty, personal appearance. This triggers sexual impulse. Each, now, desire to be with the other, to talk with the other, and touch the other. They begin to talk "openly" to each other about their thoughts and feelings. This intimacy brings an illusion of closeness, of oneness. When they are not together, they think of the other, and want to be with them. The parties feel incomplete without the other, and the other for each is the motivation for living. Being unhappy when apart, the concept of "love" arises. They think that they shall be happy together, and marry.

Westermarck:

> The sexual impulse also endangers marriage through its deceitfulness: even when raised to the rank of love it frequently leads to early marriages that soon come to an unhappy end. It is not quite so blind as it is proverbially said to be. It is stimulated by useful qualities in the opposite sex: by physical beauty which implies the full and healthy development of those visible properties that are essential to the human organism, or to the sex, or to the race. They are all the outward manifestations of physical perfection or fitness, and the instinctive preference for them is therefore evidently within the power of natural selection. But they are useful in connection with the propagation of the species, as tending to produce a vigorous and healthy offspring; on the other hand, they are no guarantees for lasting unions between the sexes. Personal appearance may also excite the sexual instinct as expression of mental qualities; emo-

> tional, moral, and intellectual qualities may act as stimulants, by evoking affection, approbation, or admiration. But under the influence of an impetuous sexual impulse such qualities are easily exaggerated beyond all reason, and the beloved person acquires, in the imagination of the lover, an immeasurable superiority over all others. **He is seen, not as he is, but as he appears irradiated by a delusive light.** (emphasis added) op. cit. p. 51, 52.

Each is mesmerized by an "image" (not the actual person) each sees in the other, and it is the "image" that each has of the other that is "desired"—not the person.

This "emotion (infatuation)," on which most marriages and intimate relationships are formed is, usually, referred to as "romantic love." It is, in the generally accepted sense, an acute preoccupation with self; a self-serving emotional attachment that is, basically, a one-way street for each—that is, each finds a temporary satisfaction through the other but without regard for the other, with an illusion of permanency, togetherness and a common goal. By the societal concept, it is something one "falls in."

Fromm pointed out:

> Frequently, of course, the "magic helper" is personified: he is conceived of as God, as principle, or as real persons such as one's parent, husband, wife, or superior . . . This process of personification of the magic helper is to be observed frequently in what is called "falling in love."
>
> —*Escape From Freedom*, p. 196, 197

Essentially, "romantic love" is an extravagantly foolish or unreasoning passion **that has not** considered intelligence, temperaments, habits, tastes, etc., and is nothing more than "desire," as that word is defined:

> That feeling or emotion which is directed to the attainment or pos-

session of some object from which pleasure or satisfaction is expected.

The "image" (not the person) being that which each needs to feel an "identity and to feel secure"—to be saved from the despair of aloneness. The "image" (not the person) is seen as the missing piece which will bring happiness.

From the poem "Masquerade" in *How I Got Ovah*, by Carolyn M. Rogers:

you think you
need me. think
that I
will complete some picture for you.

"Ritual Marriage," they feel, will bring happiness. But, any relationship can only be as lasting as the foundation on which it is formed. The concept of "love" which has arisen is irrational. Being irrational, it is short-lived because it is illusory in that each sees in the other qualities of character that do not exist. The panacea that is envisioned by the parties for marriage presumes a relationship that does not exist.

Montaigne writes:

> I see no marriages where the conjugal intelligence sooner fails, than those that we contract upon the account of beauty and amorous desires; there should be more solid and constant foundation, and they should proceed with greater circumspection; this furious ardour is worth nothing. Those who think they honour marriage by joining love to it, do, methinks, like those who, to favour virtue, hold that nobility is nothing else but virtue.
> —Book III. ch. 5 (English Translation, III. [London, 1877] p. 84)

Marriage, generally speaking, is a narcissistic ritual devoid of reason; it is a fusion without integrity, and at the core of the union is the seed of rot—pseudomorphosis—a false formation—mated but not matched.

While parties are not aware of such, they mistake "desire" for "love."

This is, also, a societal problem.

In reality, the word "love" is so commonly and universally used that it carries no specific meaning. It has been defined as a "sentiment" with certain characteristics; an "emotion," as fear or anger; a "social relationship," a condition of "rapport," "a complicated group of feelings, coupled with normal and abnormal emotions," or "a feeling accompanying an interpersonal relationship that is mutually ego enhancing." The only exact meaning that the word "love" has is a zero score in the game of tennis.

As it is used to describe a relationship between people, the most that can be said is that it conveys a meaning of something that is "pleasing." "Love" can be true, normal, abnormal, neurotic, an emotion, a science, an art, romantic, brotherly, sisterly, motherly, fatherly, erratic, understanding, sexual, sexual desire, irrational, a phenomenon, mutual sexual satisfaction, security, idolatrous, sentimental, or a host of other designations depending on whom you are reading, studying or talking to.

Additionally, you can "make love" (copulate); "fall in love"; "fall out of love" or "love can cool," dissipate. Also, it may not "run smoothly."

To understand the confusion in the concept of "love" rampant in society, it is necessary to look at the maturation process of the infant homo sapien. The confusion flows from the "natural state of childhood," a state of total dependency. The infant homo sapien, beginning with the fertilization of the egg, must depend on an external source (mother, initially) to provide the necessary essentials to sustain life—i.e., food, clothing, shelter. It is in the supplying of the essentials to sustain life that the concept of "love" arises. The "essentials to sustain life" are more than of a physical nature—i.e., food, clothing, shelter, medical, etc. There must be included the "giving" of "affection": holding, hugging, kissing and various other ways of "giving" affection.

In this environment, the child finds security. As the child grows older, and becomes aware of the surroundings, the "giving" of the essentials to sustain life is translated into the concept of "caring (love)." Those who are "giving" the essentials and affection are considered to "care" for it personally. To "give" is to "love"—i.e., gifts, in any form, are evidence of love, caring. In the developing years, the young homo sapien is in an "emotional state" that expects the essentials to sustain life (food, clothing, shelter, and even affection) to be supplied from the external source as a matter of right—merit is not a factor, whether or not supplying the essentials and affection were deserved. This is the "taking mode."

So, essentially, the societal concept of "love" is a product of the child's mind, formed in a state of dependency (one not able to exist or sustain the self without extraneous assistance), and from the effects of the relationship—basically, parent and child. The immature homo sapien is not aware that such were supplied, partially coerced in some degree, from a legal and social expectation of those who were responsible for its care or that the affection it experienced, generally speaking, was most often primarily for the benefit of the benefactor. And herein lies the fallacy of the concept of "love" as it is commonly conceived.

So, from this environment, the societal concept of "Love" is born. Yet, the societal concept of "love," generally, actually refers to the "effects" of being taken care of. It is unilateral (one-way), and such "effects" are as perceived by the mind of a "dependent"—i.e., the person "loved" is expected to be "key to happiness."

In later life, this becomes "romantic love."

In Western countries stress has been placed upon love as the bond to make a marriage. The origin for this is really unknown. In Eastern countries this concept is viewed with doubtfulness by many.

Essentially, “love” and “desire” are as opposite as day and night, light and dark. Yet, they are constantly confused. There are some generalities that can be made to distinguish between “love” and “desire”: love flows from a state of independency; desire flows from a state of dependency: love is satisfied and enriched by giving; desire takes and cannot be satisfied: love seeks to help; desire seeks to be helped: love moves cautiously; desire travels blindly: love radiates in all direction, and desire moves in but one.

Ignorance

It is necessary to repeat what has been previously stated.

What is the common process of marriage?

> A youth and maiden, meeting by chance, are brought together by artifice, exchange glances, reciprocate civilities, go home and dream of one another. Having little to divert attention, or diversify a thought, they find themselves uneasy when they are apart, and therefore conclude that they shall be happy together.
>
> —*Rasselas*, Johnson, XXIX

They let it be known that they intend to get married.

Marriage—the act of joining as husband and wife—is generally spoken of as a civil contract. A contract requires mutual consent—a meeting of the minds—which means that each has the mental capacity to understand, and does understand what is being done and what is involved. In other words, they are aware, have knowledge of, the duties, responsibilities, expectations and all the significance of the act of marriage.

The questions, then, (1) Do the parties have the mental capacity to make an informed decision?, and (2) Are the parties sufficiently aware of the intricacies of the involvement of marriage to make an informed decision?

To answer these questions, it is necessary to know what marriage is.

So, what is marriage?

The "honorable state of matrimony" is in part:

a legal entity, there are certain rights, duties, responsibilities and privileges after the joining as man and wife. It is also the means for the determination of privileges and responsibilities in the use and distribution of property;

a social unit, as it becomes a "cell" of the body of the culture of which it is a part with the attending responsibility as an "agent" of that culture to help organize and control societal behavior to achieve enlightenment;

a psychological challenge, within the relationship of the parties, many adjustments of attitude must be made by each, and making adjustments will continue during the entire relationship. In addition, there are relationships of friends, relatives, and business associates for which an accommodation must be made. Further, there must be a balancing of individual careers with family life, and, ultimately, usually, children that must be dealt with;

a philosophical school, not only must the parties have some standard of reference (a philosophy) to determine their various decisions and activities, but, again, there will be, usually, children that must be taught; and, always, the choice of religious beliefs;

an economic partnership, the "family" is the *centerpiece* of the culture. All activities of the culture relate directly to the "family." Business, schools, religious organizations and cultural activities are sustained by the *family*: all are seeking a portion of the disposal income. The various decisions concerning the payment of the essentials (mortgage, rent, utilities, etc.) and purchasing of food, clothes, cars, furniture, etc. are often overwhelming. Since young married couples are vulnerable in business affairs and a favorite prey for the "business vultures" of society, the economy of the home becomes the most disruptive, causing many arguments; and,

a political unit, which is as important as the **economic partnership** since the very foundation of government (county, city, state and federal) is dependent on an understanding of the political systems and an active participation by the parties. There is a thread that touches all members of society that requires everyone to understand that it is the responsibility of every individual to act in such a way that the government (city, county, state and federal) is to serve ALL THE PEOPLE (of the people, by the people and for the people). Further, that the primary purpose of government is to provide an environment in which everyone can safely pursuit their individual goal of life, liberty and the pursuit of happiness.

Having viewed the honorable state of matrimony, it is necessary to look at the preparations that have been made for this momentous journey before we can answer the questions that were put forth.

First, Do the parties have the mental capacity to make an informed decision?

No. It is impossible for the essential element of a contract—consent, meaning knowledge of and appreciation of the involvement—to be present. The marriage, generally speaking, will begin with the relationship on an "illusory high." In this euphoric state, there is only short term planning; each enters into the union for the purpose of achieving or fulfilling some felt personal immediate need or goal which is expected to be accomplished through the other, which translates into "love" for each other, as avowed by the parties. Even though it is spoken by both parties that the vows are to create a permanent relationship, they are blinded by the ardor of desire. In reality, the future of the relationship has not been considered.

Are the parties sufficiently aware of the intricacies of the involvement of marriage to make an informed decision?

Let us look at the situation from the standpoint of "generally speaking."

Have either of them given thought to goals in life, gender, having and raising children, religious beliefs, etc.?

No.

Have they been instructed on the selection of a mate?
No.

Do they know why they are attracted to each other?
No.

Have the parties looked at each other with a critical eye?
No.

Have they discussed their thoughts and feeling about goals in life, gender, having and raising children, religious beliefs, etc.?
No.

Have they been instructed as to purpose and meaning of marriage?
No.

Have they been instructed on the intricacies of the involvement of marriage?
No.

Have they been instructed on the bearing, rearing and education of children?
No.

Have they been instructed on the economics of the home?
No.

Have they been made aware of the mandatory personal adjustments that must be made?
No.

Do the parties have a full understanding of what is involved when the vows are spoken?

No.

What preparations were made for this momentous journey? None.

The parties are, essentially, in a "state of ignorance," of themselves, of the other, of their feelings for the other and of that which they are entering. As the "avowals of love" are given in a "state of ignorance," so, too, the marriage vows. They will be built on quicksand. The relationship, "like the best efforts of man, however glorious the early results, will have a dismal ending—like plants which put forth beautiful flowers and then grow rank and coarse and wither."

It is their ignorance of themselves and of each other that "separateness in marriage" will become the essence of the relationship. Mated but not matched. "Separateness," in this circumstance, is a means of survival—the only way the parties can continue to live together. It is an accommodation for ignorance and fear, an effort to make the best of a hopeless situation. It is an effort to make "a silk purse (good marriage) out of a sow's ear (incompatibility)."

And while this is simplistic, it contains the essence of most marriages that are entered into for "love."

Contrary Purposes

Man's love is of man's life a part;
It is woman's whole existence.

—Byron

A practical description:

Marriage, for years, has been, is, a public ritual by which a woman (thinks she) finds love, and a man (thinks he) gains convenience (sex, cook, maid, and, more recently, another paycheck) and social acceptance. The ritual began, and continues, on these assumptions: (1) that man is superior to woman; that woman's role is to serve man (which includes bearing and rearing man's children); that man, being magnanimous, having been formed in the image of God, will provide the woman and child(ren) the necessities for sustaining life. Then, strong in their relationship, begin pursuit of the realities of life (wealth, power, fame), with children being evidence to the world of a very close relationship (eat your heart out world), or negligence (we really wanted eight), knowing "what God (magistrate, Probate Judge, Notary Public) hath put together, no man (lawyer not included) can put asunder." And on this foundation, it all begins—and ends.

While the attachment of a woman to a man in an intimate-personal relationship (marriage) is translated into "love" on the surface, it is more. The bond between husband and wife is far more important, of a greater magnitude, and of a different aspect, generally speaking, for the woman than the man. With the woman, there is a fusion with the man psychologically that results in "oneness"; it is, almost, as if the two were tethered—an invisible umbilical connection. The man becomes her "alter ego," and, thereafter, the woman gets from the man her security, affection, identity, and direction (SAID/LOVE) and, thereby, achieves emotional and psychological "existence," just as the fetus depends on the woman for physical existence. So strongly and metaphysically does a woman take the vows of marriage that her own individuality is merged into her husband's and her free will receives a mortal blow. It is a necessary part of the fusion process for the woman to feel that the man cares for her "personally." After the attachment, woman does not have an existence, psychologically, apart from the man. This is the "beginning" for her; it is, probably, the most significant event in her life.

Lust, thro' some certain strainers well refin'd,
Is gentle love, and claims all womankind.

—Anonymous

To understand the Umbilical Connection, it is necessary to look to the past.

In all of recorded history, for most cultures, woman has never been considered as an equal of man; always something less than man, inferior to man.

"Hast thou not made me here thy substitute,
"And these inferior far beneath me set?
"Among *unequals* what society
"Can sort, what harmony or true delight?
"Which must be mutual, in proportion due
"Giv'n and receiv'd; but in *disparity*
"The one intense, the other still remiss
"Cannot well suit with either, but soon prove
"Tedious alike: of *fellowship* I speak
"Such as I seek, fit to participate
"All rational delight"

—*Paradise Lost VIII*, pp. 391–92, Milton

Woman was, essentially, an object for use by the man. Her status was similar to that of a slave.

In Greek mythology, it was the usual for the woman to be abducted and raped. Even Zeus, the supreme ruler, took his sexual pleasures at will without regard for the consequences to the woman—Io, Europa, Danae, Leto—to name a few; so, to, other gods: Persephone by Hades, Creusa, when hardly more than a child, by Apollo, Orithyia, by Boreas—to name a few.

She has been used in all segments of society by the man, historically, as the bait, the object, the trophy, the decoration, the honey, the prize, the chattel, the instrument of life, and the oil for the wheel of his machinations: by the king for acquisition, stability, alliance, continuity; by the wealthy to merge fortunes and to preserve prestige and position; by the poor to attain wealth and prestige.

Even in some modern wedding vows, the question is still asked, "Who gives away this woman?", and many of these beliefs (illusions) remain with us today—certainly, psychologically, if not legally.

A woman has been culturally deprived of an independent psychological identity, that is, a separate existence apart from the man, for so long that she has accepted this void, and her separate existence has almost become biologically extinct. SHE GIVES UP THE INDEPENDENCE OF HER INDIVIDUAL SELF AND FUSES IT WITH HER HUSBAND, OR SIGNIFICANT MALE COMPANION, IN ORDER TO ACQUIRE THE STRENGTH WHICH SHE ACCEPTED WAS LACKING IN HER SELF.

The psychological aspect is succinctly stated by Fromm:

> . . . There is, however, a milder form of dependency which is so general in our culture that only in exceptional cases does it seem to be lacking. . . .
>
> I am referring to the kind of person whose whole life is in a

subtle way related to some power outside themselves. There is nothing they do, feel, or think which is not somehow related to this power. They expect protection from "him," wish to be taken care of by "him," make "him" also responsible for whatever may be the outcome of their own actions. Often the fact of his dependence is something the person is not aware of at all . . . There is no definite image linked up with that power. Its essential quality is to represent a certain function, namely to protect, help, and develop the individual, to be with him, and never leave him alone. The "X" which has these qualities may be called the magic helper. Frequently, of course, the "magic helper" is personified: he is conceived of as God, as principle, or as real persons such as one's parent, husband, wife, or superior. . . . This process of personification of the magic helper is to be observed frequently in what is called "falling in love."

—*Escape From Freedom*, p. 196, 197

Jean Kerr:

It is easier to live through someone else than to become complete yourself.

—*The Snake Has All The Lines.*

For the man, marriage carries the illusion of his being a stable, responsible person, and is the socially acceptable way for him to gratify his sexual desire. "Love," generally speaking, is totally related to "power" and "convenience." He does not feel the relatedness to woman as the woman feels toward him; there is no fusion of identity as with the woman. The man's concept of oneness is the same as "possession." But, he is aware of the expectations of society.

Male Superiority

The traditional hierarchical family, as it has been celebrated in most cultures for centuries, and, specifically the western culture, such as the family of Jesus, teaches authoritarian patterns and a belief in the unchanging rightness of male power. Since the beginning of recorded history, the rightness of male power has permeated the Institution of Marriage.

In early Rome, a man could repudiate his wife without giving any reason but such was not available to the woman. Cato said of divorce:

> If you find your wife in the act of adultery, the law permits you to kill her without trial. If she surprises you in the same condition, she must not touch you even with the tips of her fingers; the law forbids her.

And that ascribed to Demosthenes in oration against Neasia:

> We keep mistresses for our pleasures, concubines for constant attendance, and wives to bear us legitimate children and to be our faithful housekeepers.

Very early, these beliefs were mirrored in religious concepts.

> Unto the woman he said, I will greatly multiply thy sorrow and thy conception; in sorrow thou shalt bring forth children; and **thy desire shall be to thy husband, and he shall rule over thee**. (emphasis added)
>
> —*Genesis* 3, v16

A view of the same from Elizabeth Cady Stanton—a woman's perspective:

> The Bible teaches that woman brought sin and death into the world, that she precipitated the fall of the race, that she was arraigned before the judgment seat of Heaven, tried, condemned and sentenced. Marriage for her was to be a condition of bondage, maternity a period of suffering and anguish, and in silence and subjection, she was to play the role of a dependant on man's bounty for all her material wants.
>
> —*The Woman's Bible*, Pt. I, p. 1895

The significance of male power is very simple: woman is inferior to man.

"A woman without ability is normal," said the Chinese.

According to the Hindus and Judeo Christian concept, ". . . infidelity, violence, deceit, envy, extreme avarice, a total want of good qualities, with impurities" were the natural faults of women.

This attitude is reflected in the societal belief, until a moment ago, historically, that the woman did not have the aptitude to be educated; they were too weak to stand the strain of serious mental labor.

Since the beginning of recorded history in the Western cultures, the rightness of male power has permeated the Institution of Marriage. Love and power are linked, which means marriage has been dominated by the husband. Very early, these beliefs (illusions) were mirrored in religious concepts, and became a part of the common law. The common law was, practically, a restatement of the customs then prevailing.

After marriage, husband and wife became one person, legally. That is, the identity of the wife was merged into that of the husband under whose cover she was, and was called *feme covert*. A wife could not dispose of property, make a will or contract, commit a tort or be sued in her own name—she became a nonentity. It was assumed that the wife had no independent will, but acted under the domination and control of the husband.

This belief arises out of the biblical concept that woman, having been formed from one of man's ribs, was an appendage of man—his helpmate and inferior.

> Unto the woman he said, I will greatly multiply thy sorrow and thy conception; in sorrow thou shalt bring forth children; and **thy desire shall be to thy husband, and he shall rule over thee**. (emphasis added)
>
> —*Genesis* 3, v16

When confronted with his misdeeds, Bumble, in the manner of his first ancestor, Adam, blamed his wife:

> "That is no excuse," replied Mr. Bownlow. "You . . . are the more guilty of the two, in the eye of the law; for the law supposes that your wife acts under your direction."
> "If the law supposes that," said Mr. Bumble, squeezing his hat emphatically in both hands, "the law is an ass—an idiot."
>
> —Charles Dickens, *The Adventures of Oliver Twist*, p. 333 (London, 1914)

In this relationship, generally, the man provided the living and the wife took care of the home and children.

Mary Bokin Chesnut:

> You know how women sell themselves and are sold in marriage, from queens downwards, eh? You know what the Bible says about slaves, and marriage. Poor women, poor slaves.
>
> —*Diary from Dixie* (March 4, 1861), p. 1949

John Mills:

> . . . when a woman marries, it may in general be understood that

she makes choice of the management of a household, and the bringing up of a family, as the first call upon her exertions, during as many years of her life as may be required for the purpose; and that she renounces, not all other objects and occupations, but all which are not consistent with the requirements of this.

—*The Subjection of Women*, p. 295.

Susan B. Anthony:

Of all the old prejudices that cling to the hem of the woman's garment and persistently impede her progress, none holds faster than this. The idea that she owes service to a man instead of to herself, and that it is her highest duty to aid his development rather than her own, will be the last to die.

—*The Status of Women, Past, Present and Future, The Arena*, May 1897.

Emma Goldman:

And yet we find many emancipated women who prefer marriage, with all its deficiencies, to the narrowness of an unmarried life; narrow and unendurable because of the chains of moral and social prejudice that cramp and bind her nature.

—*The Tragedy of Women's Emancipation, Anarchism and Other Essays*, p. 1911.

But, there is more.

Love and power are linked. With the right of control, came the right to punish and restrain. As part of his right to punish and restrain the wife to compel obedience, the husband could chastise the wife. The definition of "chastise" being: to punish, esp. by beating; to scold or criticize severely.

This right of the husband was succinctly stated, poetically, by an early English writer:

> "God has given the man greater wit, better strength, better courage, to compel the woman to obey, by reason or force . . ."
>
> —Sir Thomas Smith

Of course, the husband was expected to exercise this "right" moderately. If the husband became "overzealous" in "chastising," the courts would only interfere in "serious" cases (permanent injury or an excess of violence) since "domestic broils" were of a "trivial nature" and best left to family government (husband). For this "wholesome exercise" he could use a stick as big as his thumb. Significantly, a letter to the *Realm* magazine, August 2002, page 63, from a reader, relates some confusion relating to the right of a husband to beat his wife:

> RULE OF THUMB?
>
> I thought your readers might be interested to learn of a dispute over the origin of the phrase "rule of thumb." It is thought to have derived from the ancient right of a husband allowing him to beat his wife so long as he used a stick that was no thicker than his thumb.
>
> There is plenty of documentary evidence for the existence of this law, not least various contemporary cartoons. The most famous, by Rowlandson, was published in 1782 (right). The judge carries a bundle of sticks, each with a thumb carved into the end. The rule is also documented in the *Law of Women*, used in England until the 1500s: "A man may beat a woman with a stick or rod as thick as his middle finger and as long as his forearm."
>
> Whether the rule of thumb was used after the 16th century is debatable. Christina Hoff Sommers explains a recent theory in her book *Who Stole Feminism*? The phrase is thought to have come from a method of estimating length, originally used by wood workers measuring with their thumbs.
>
> It seems that while the old "wife beating" rule involved a thumb, it was not the origin of the phrase "rule of thumb."

Violence to the woman is a cultural tradition.

> Thou goest to women? Do not forget thy whip!
> —*Thus Spake Zarathustra*, Nietzsche.

While the right of a husband to chastise the wife to compel obedience has not been legally sanctioned for years, societal customs are hard to break, as is evidenced by the present violence to women.

Generally speaking, most abuse, physical and psychological, to the woman by the man, occurs only after the parties have been married for a period of time.

Again, we go to Cervantes:

> Now, love in young men is not love but lust, and as its ultimate end is pleasure, it ceases once that subject has been attained; and what appeared to be love must disappear because it cannot pass the limits assigned to it by nature, whereas true affection knows none of such limitations. I mean to say that no sooner had Don Fernando enjoyed the farmer's daughter than his desires weakened and his amorous impulses cooled. If at first he had pretended that he would absent himself in order to get rid of his passions, he now earnestly endeavoured to go away to avoid fulfilling his promises.
> —*Don Quixote*

But there are many times abuse occurs in an outburst of anger, ignited by resentment and inflamed by alcohol, a response to an immediate ego threatening situation or an unwanted demand.

From the woman, where there was the accolade of the "lover," there are now the lamentations of the abused and neglected wife, as Tennyson observed:

> He will hold thee, when his passion
> shall have spent its novel force,
> Something better than his dog, a little
> dearer than his horse.
>
> —*Locksley Hall*

The observation of Judge Caldwell explains the phenomenon:

The rule is without exception that whenever the exclusive power of making or administering the law (home) is committed for any extended period to a single man (husband) or a few men—to a caste—the progressive restriction of the liberty of the people (wife and children) follow.

This seems to be an international phenomenon.
Listen . . .
From America . . .
Faulkner:

Hitting a woman don't hurt her because a woman don't shove back at a lick like a man do: she just gives to it and then when your back is turned, reaches for the flat-iron or the butcher knife. That's why hitting them don't break nothing; all it does is just black her eye or cut her mouf a little, and that ain't nothing to a woman. Because why? Because what better sign than a black eye or a cut mouf can a woman want from a man that he got her on his mind?

—*The Reivers*, p. 263

From France . . .
Moliere:

Act 1 Scene 1

Sganarelle (husband of Martine), Martine (wife of Sganarelle) enter quarreling.
SGANARELLE. No, I tell you I won't do anything of the sort, and I'm the one to say and be the master.
MARTINE. And I tell you that I want you to live to suit me, and I didn't marry you to put up with your carryings-on.

SGANARELLE. Oh, what a weary business it is to have a wife, and how right Aristotle is when he says a wife is worse than a demon!

MARTINE. Just listen to that smart fellow with his half-wit Aristotle!

SGANARELLE. Yes, a smart fellow. Just find me a woodcutter who knows how to reason about things, like me, who served a famous doctor for six years, and who as a youngster knew his elementary Latin book by heart.

MARTINE. A plague on the crazy fool!

SGANARELLE. A plague on the slut!

MARTINE. Cursed be the day when I went and said yes!

SGANARELLE. Cursed be the hornified notary who had me sign my own ruin!

MARTINE. Really, it's a fine thing for you to complain of that affair! Should you let a single moment go by without thanking Heaven for having me for your wife? And did you deserve to marry a person like me?

SGANARELLE. Oh, yes, you did me too much honor, and I had reason to congratulate myself on our wedding night! Oh, my Lord! Don't get me started on that! I'd have a few things to say . . .

MARTINE. What? What would you say?

SGANARELLE. Let it go at that; let's drop that subject. Enough that we know what we know, and that you were very lucky to find me.

MARTINE. What do you mean, lucky to find you? A man who drags me down to the poorhouse, a debauchee, a traitor, who eats up everything I own?

SGANARELLE. That's a lie: I drink part of it.

MARTINE. Who sells, piece by piece, everything in the house.

SGANARELLE. That's living on our means.

MARTINE. Who's taken even my bed from under me.

SGANARELLE. You'll get up all the earlier in the morning.

MARTINE. In short, who doesn't leave a stick of furniture in the whole house.

SGANARELLE. All the easier to move out.

MARTINE. And who does nothing but gamble and drink from morning to night.
SGANARELLE. That's so I won't get bored.
MARTINE. And what do you expect me to do with my family in the meantime?
SGANARELLE. Whatever you like.
MARTINE. I have four poor little children on my hands.
SGANARELLE. Set them on the floor.
MARTINE. Who are constantly asking me for bread.
SGANARELLE. Give them the whip. When I've had plenty to eat and drink, I want everyone in my house to have his fill.
MARTINE. And you, you drunkard, do you expect things to go on forever like this?
SGANARELLE. My good wife, let's go easy, if you please.
MARTINE. And me to endure your insolence and debauchery to all eternity?
SGANARELLE. Let's not get excited, my good wife.
MARTINE. And that I can't find a way to make you do your duty?
SGANARELLE. My good wife, you know that my soul isn't very patient and my arm is pretty good.
MARTINE. You make me laugh with your threats.
SGANARELLE. My good little wife, my love, you're itching for trouble, as usual.
MARTINE. I'll show you I'm not afraid of you.
SGANARELLE. My dear better half, you're asking for something.
MARTINE. Do you think your words frighten me?
SGANARELLE. Sweet object of my eternal vows, I'll box your ears.
MARTINE. Drunkard that you are!
SGANARELLE. I'll beat you.
MARTINE. Wine sack!
SGANARELLE. I'll wallop you.
MARTINE. Wretch!
SGANARELLE. I'll tan your hide.
MARTINE. Traitor, wiseacre, deceiver, coward, scoundrel, gallowsbird, beggar, good-for-nothing, rascal, villain, thief.

SGANARELLE. (takes a stick and beats her). Ah! So you want it, eh?
MARTINE. Oh, oh, oh, oh!
SGANARELLE. That's the right way to pacify you.

—*The Doctor In Spite of Himself*

From France . . . Heloise . . .

Tell me one thing, and here she drove her dart:
Why, after our conversion, commanded by thyself, did I drop into oblivion, to be no more refreshed by speech of thine or letter? Tell me, I say, if you can, or I will say what I feel and what everyone suspects: desire rather than friendship drew you to me, lust rather than love. So when desire ceased, whatever you were manifesting for its sake likewise vanished. This, beloved, is not so much my opinion as the opinion of all. Would it were only mine and that thy love might find defenders to argue away my pain. Would that I could invent some reason to excuse you and also cover my cheapness. Listen, I beg, to what I ask, and it will seem small and very easy to you. Since I am cheated of your presence, at least put vows in words, of which you have a store, and so keep before me the sweetness of thine image . . . When little more than a girl I took the hard vows of a nun, not from piety but at your command. If I merit nothing from thee, how vain I deem my labor! I can expect no reward from God, as I have done nothing from love of Him . . . God knows, at your command I would have followed or preceded you to fiery places. For my heart is not with me, but with thee.

From China . . .

A Complaint

He lodged us in a spacious house,
And plenteous was our fare.
But now at every frugal meal
There's not a scrap to spare.
Alas! alas that this good man
Could not go on as he begun!

(Some verses of)

The Plaint of King Yew's Forsaken Wife

The fibres of the white flowered rush
Are with the white grass bound.
So do the two together go,
In closest union found.
And thus should man and wife abide,
The twain combined in one;
But this bad man sends me away,
And bids me dwell alone.

The mulberry branches they collect,
And use their food to cook;
But I must use a furnace small,
That pot nor pan will brook.
So me that great man badly treats,
Nor uses as his wife,
Degrades me from my proper place,
And fills with grief my life.

The yellow ducks sit on the dam,
With left wing gathered low;
So on each other do they lean,
And their attachment show.

And love should thus the man and wife
In closest concord bind;
But that man turns away from me,
And shows a fickle mind.

(Some verses of)

The Plaint of a Rejected Wife

The east wind gently blows,
With cloudy skies and rain.
'Twixt man and wife should ne'er be strife,
But harmony obtain.

Radish and mustard plaints
Are used, though some be poor;
While my good name is free from blame,
Don't thrust me from your door.

No cherishing you give,
I'm hostile in your eyes.
As peddler's wares for which none cares,
My virtues you despise.

When poverty was nigh,
I strove our means to spare;
You, now rich grown, me scorn to own;
To poison me compare.

The stores for winter piled
Are all unprized in spring.
No now, elate with your new mate,
Myself away you fling.

Your cool disdain for me
    A bitter anguish hath.
The early time, our love's sweet prime,
    In you wakes only wrath.

If the husband became "overzealous" in "chastising," the courts would only interfere in "serious" cases (permanent injury or an excess of violence) since "domestic broils" were of a "trivial nature" and best left to family government (husband), as was previously stated.

Here, an illustration:

> Wife files for divorce on ground of physical cruelty. The marriage was for 9 years before separation; there were two children of marriage. Wife testified that the husband kicked her in stomach while pregnant; had knocked her down and stomped her in the face; that he beat her, on one occasion, to such an extent that her neck was stiff for two weeks and required medical attention; that on at least a half dozen other instances he beat and choked her and that she was bruised after some of the numerous severe beatings.

The husband denied the accusations.

Judgment of Court (all men): Divorce Refused.

It is not every slight violence, however, committed by the husband, or wife against the other, even in anger, which will authorize the divorce.

Courts are loath to grant a divorce for a single act of physical violence.

> **Continued acts** of personal violence producing physical pain or bodily injury **and a fear of future danger** are recognized as sufficient cause for divorce for cruelty in nearly all jurisdictions, **especially where accompanied by other acts of ill treatment**. (emphasis added)
>
> Physical cruelty, as used in divorce law, has generally been

> defined by our courts as actual personal violence or such a course of physical treatment as endangers life, limb or health, and renders cohabitation unsafe.
>
> —*Crowder v. Crowder*, 143 S.E.2nd 580, 583, 1965

It seems to be obvious that the past still influences the present with many husbands still abusing their wives and children, a learned response from the past when it was an acceptable mode of behavior by society, regarded as part of love and marriage. This is, also, why husbands, when given a choice, prefer the ground of "physical cruelty" to be the ground used in an action for a divorce against them by their wife. The acceptance by society of the violence by the husband to the wife and children without stigma is the prime factor for the phenomenon.

Religious Dogma

The religious dogmas of "what God has joined together, let no man put asunder," and that the female was made from a male rib were obviously constructed by males since the ultimate effect is to encourage the physical and mental abuse of the female by the male and exploit her energy.

The contradiction and prejudice against women is obvious in the following passages:

Jonathan Swift:

> What they do in heaven we are ignorant of; but what they do not we are told expressly, that they neither marry nor are given in marriage.
>
> —*Thoughts on Various Subjects*

> For in the resurrection they neither marry, nor are given in marriage.
>
> —*Matthew 22–30*

> For when they shall rise from the dead, they neither marry, nor are given in marriage.
>
> —*Mark* 12:25

> They which shall be accounted worthy to obtain that world, and the resurrection from the dead, neither marry, nor are given in marriage.
>
> —*Luke* 20:35

The Child

For centuries, and presently for the most part, the infant homo sapien becomes a part of an environment, the home usually, in which the thoughts and actions of the care-givers, usually parents, were, and are, primarily, dominated by "emotions"—a barren soil.

In this environment, the child is given little support in developing security, intelligence, relationships, personality, creativity, character and values. These care-givers bind the emotional and intellectual growth of their children in the chains of their beliefs and religious myths as effectively as the ancient Chinese bound the feet of the female child to prevent the growth of her feet. The children in these relationships have been, and are, subjected to an environment from birth in the home, in entertainment, business and government, that is stressful and oppressive; there has been, and is, inconsistency, violence and discord. Further, children have been confronted, too often, with an attitude from the parents, or caregivers, of indifference, isolation, domination, tolerance, intolerance, indifference, apathy, disinterest, insensibility, nonchalance, hatred, repugnance, hostility or loathing. They have been, generally speaking, the pawns of parents who are, and were, ignorant and indifferent to the needs of the child's being, or the needs of the children were secondary to the desire of the parent to create the child in an image of their shadow or used to fulfill unrealized ambitions, and viewed simply as a by-product of a relationship, or a means to save a marriage, or an object for a parent to enhance an ego, or a myriad of other uses—rarely as a **homo sapien**.

Sometimes, it is even admitted:

Dear Abby: I am a wife and the mother of three healthy, active children, ages 8, 6 and 3½.

I am short-tempered and easily angered, but get over it quickly. I sent for your booklet "The Anger In All of Us, and How to Deal With It," and I learned a great deal from it.

This paragraph describes me perfectly:

I doubt if there is a mother alive who has not done or said something to her child in anger. One need not lift a hand to hurt a child. Words can cut as sharply as a knife, ("I hate you!" "You are stupid!" "I wish you had never been born!")

Abby, I actually screamed those very words at my 8-year-old son. I used some of your suggestions on how to control my temper. At first, I thought they were too simplistic, but I put them to use when I felt I was "losing it." I put my hands over my mouth, took a deep breath and slowly counted to 10. It calmed me down and kept me from hitting my 6-year-old.

Another time, I phoned my best friend and told her I was angry at my kids and called her to help me cool off. She laughed and said, "Keep talking, honey. I may call YOU when one of my kids makes me crazy!"

Abby, I just had to write to tell you that your anger booklet has been a lifesaver for me. If you print this, please don't use my name. My husband is a pediatrician.

—*Anderson Independent-Mail*, Sunday, October 9, 1994, 3D.

And, what is the dominant societal philosophy to which the homo sapien youth is exposed?

Power, wealth and fame!

There is a shrine to these "Gods" in almost every home. Education, the key to an enlightened culture, is given only "lip service," and is only one means of attaining one, or all, of the dominant societal goals!

And, then, there is that ubiquitous illusory philosophy that permeates all of society, social, business and religion: male superiority!

The observation of Mills regarding such explains much of why society is as it is:

> All the selfish propensities, the self worship, the unjust self-preference, which exist among mankind, have their source in, and derive their principal nourishment from, the present constitution of the relation between man and woman. Think what it is to a boy, to grow up to manhood in the belief that without any merit or any exertion of his own, though he may be the most frivolous and empty or the most ignorant and stolid of mankind, by the mere fact of being born a male he is by right the superior of all and every one of an entire half of the human race: including probably some whose real superiority to himself he has daily or hourly occasion to feel; but even if in his whole conduct he habitually follows a woman's guidance, still, if he is a fool, thinks that of course she is not, and cannot be, equal in ability and judgment to himself; and if he is not a fool, he does worse—he sees that she is superior to him, and believes that, notwithstanding her superiority, he is entitled to command and she is bound to obey. What must be the effect on his character, of **this lesson**?
>
> . . . Is it imagined that all this does not pervert the whole manner of existence of the man, both as an individual and as a social being?
>
> —*The Subjection of Women*, p. 354–56.

Or the woman?

The enfant female homo sapien gets a "double whammy." In addition to the necessary state of dependency for survival, resulting from the nature of creation, in which she is born, she is taught that she is "dependent on" and "something less than" the male homo sapien.

When the whole manner of existence of the man (and the woman) is perverted, both as an individual and as a social being, society, as a whole, becomes perverted.

Mills pointed out in *The Subjection of Women*, p. 287:

> The family is a school of despotism, in which the virtues of despotism, but also its vices, are largely nourished.

And Hugo in *Les Miserables* (p. 494):

> All the crimes of man begin with the vagrancy of childhood.

If we consider that society requires stringent regulations for one to acquire a license to cut hair as a business, but places no regulations for one to have and raise a child, then, we must conclude that cutting hair has more value to society than having and raising a child. Further, we will not permit one to use a computer without proper training and instruction, but we will put a new life for direction and training with a child.

One can only teach what one knows. As has been noted, you cannot put a child into the hands of children and expect the children to teach the child how to be an enlightened, mature adult, as our culture has been, and is presently doing. When I speak of children, I am not talking of those persons who are chronologically under the legal age, although they are included, but of that mass of people who are chronologically considered to be an adult but are still "psychologically" immature. Neither the chronological age or formal education of an individual is an indication of the degree of "psychological" maturity. This custom, a child in the hands of children, has resulted in a dichotomous attitude by society toward the homo sapien nursling.While mankind will say that the attitude toward the **homo sapien nursling—the child**—has been one of "**love**," in the time of recorded history to the present **the child** has been treated as a toy, a plaything, a show piece, a possession, a display, an exhibit, a spectacle, a demonstration, an object by which one may achieve unrealized dreams or a centerpiece for the family, and, has been maligned, abused, used, misused, battered, mistreated, molested, ravished, violated, tormented, persecuted, deformed, disfigured, crippled, maimed, mangled and murdered.

Surely, our ACTIONS are truer than our WORDS.

Such has been recognized by the court:

> Your children have come into this world because of the two of you. Perhaps you two made lousy choices as to who you decided to be the other parent. If so, that is YOUR problem and YOUR fault.
>
> No matter what you think of the other party—or what your family thinks of the other party—those children are one half of each of you. Remember that, because every time you tell your child what an idiot his father is, or what a fool his mother is, or how bad the absent parent is, or what terrible things that person has done, you are telling the child that half of HIM is bad.
>
> That is an unforgivable thing to do to a child. That is not love; it is possession. If you do that to your children, you will destroy them as surely as if you had cut them into pieces, because that is what you are doing to their emotions.
>
> I sincerely hope you don't do that to your children. Think more about your children and less about yourselves, and make yours a selfless kind of love not foolish or selfish, or THEY will suffer.
>
> —*Anderson Independent-Mail*, id.

Interestingly, sometimes, the homo sapien youth are violent, use drugs or alcohol.

While the homo sapien youth are, essentially, tolerated and, then, abandoned, they are expected to grow up to be successful in every sense of the word. The sad fact is that the youth have been failed miserably by parents and country (society).

The "family" (married or in an intimate relationship), then, has been, and is, the soil that nourishes the growth of ignorance, which translates into violence, hate, war, selfishness, greed, envy, lust, drugs, homosexuality, and all of the catalogue of crimes, and vice—all of those events that fill the newspapers, magazines, periodicals, books and airways—all of that which society is experiencing this day, this hour.

Thus, we have two sets of "family values": the "reality"—violence, power, wealth and fame; and the "illusory"—love, togetherness and education, spoken of by religious persons and politicians.

Euthenics

> (The science and art of improving the human race through securing the best of external influences and conditions of environment for the development of the individual physically, mentally and morally, and for maintaining his vigor and his health.)

Are the past and present cultures, saturated by war, crime, hate, discord, violence and hostility, the only kind of society that mankind can hope to achieve? Do the annals of history (history being all events behind the second) depict the true capacity and nature of Man—the homo sapien?

No, to both questions.

The past is a "bucket of ashes." I am a "cock-eyed optimist."

There is a passage in Melville's *Moby Dick*, in the chapter "The Whale's Skeleton," page 349, when upon viewing the bones of one of the leviathans, he states:

> How vain and foolish, then, thought I, for timid untraveled man to try to comprehend aright this wondrous whale, by merely poring over his dead attenuated skeleton, stretched in this peaceful wood. No. Only in the heart of quickest perils; only when within the eddyings of his angry flukes; only on the profound unbounded sea, can the fully invested whale be truly and livingly found out.

As the whale cannot be comprehended aright by his skeleton, neither can Mankind be comprehended aright by its skeleton (the annals of history) or the technologies that Mankind has created and used for tremendous destruction.

Mankind does have a choice for a society different from our present culture and that reflected by the annals of history.

While war, violence, prejudice, crime, hate, poverty, divisiveness, intolerance, apathy (welfare state), etc., have been a continuing part of the annals of history, such conditions are not inherent in man's biological design—a physical and psychological mature person—a rational being—homo sapien.

If ever mankind hopes to overcome the "state of passion" in which man "wallows" and achieve that state of "enlightenment" for which man is designed (rationality), where, for the most part, there will be no violence, wife abuse, child abuse, prejudice, blind ambitions, substantial alcoholism, drug addiction, crime, war or poverty, man must untie the "knot of ignorance."

It is time for man to put the "other half" of his brain to work so that the annals of history will reflect something other than his resourcefulness in the invention of the knife, the bow and arrow, bullets, pistols, rifles, machine guns, mortars, hand grenades, fighter planes, bomber planes, bombs, lethal gas, etc.

As Marriage has been the soil that nourished the growth of violence, hate, ignorance, war, selfishness, dependency, anxiety and frustration, so it must be Marriage that carries society to enlightenment.

Why?

The relationship between husband and wife has such an influence on each that it has an effect on all their relationships: partner, family, society, work, recreation, politics and business. And it is this relationship, generally speaking, that creates the environment that will have the most influence on the development of the child, and the "child" is the "raw material" that a society must use to achieve a given culture: the "family" (society) can mold the child to produce a barbaric society, as it has done and is presently doing, or the mold can produce an enlightened society, in accordance with the design of man—*homo sapien.*

Consider the environment which the child does, and has, become a part of.

Presently, and in the past, most parties in marriage lack maturity. Essentially, they are in the "throes of passion," guided by their emotions, though chronologically and legally mature.

These care-givers can best be described with a paraphrase from the Bible, I Corinthians 13:11:

> When I was a child, I spake as a child, I understood as a child, I thought as a child; and when I became an adult, I spake as an child, I understood as a child, I thought as a child.

Such was noted by Goethe:

> All our learned teachers and educators are agreed that children do not know why they want what they want; but no one is willing to believe that adults too, like children, wander about this earth in a daze and, like children, do not know where they come from or where they are going, act as rarely as they do according to genuine motives, and are as thoroughly governed as they are by biscuits and cake and the rod.
>
> —*The Sorrows of Young Werther*, May 22.

This was also noted by T.S. Eliot:

> I don't believe one grows older. I think that what happens early on in life is that at a certain age one stands still and stagnates.[quoted in *New York Times*, Sept. 21, 1958]

Again, Hesse:

> ". . . all of the people on the street are not rational beings simply because they walk upright and females carry the young in their bodies nine months."
>
> —*Demian*, p. 89

Also, Emerson observed in the essay, *The Poet*,

> ". . . but the great majority of men seem to be minors, who have not yet come into possession of their own . . ."

And, then, there is the matter of the personality of the parties in the marriage. When the parties marry, they are, essentially, strangers. After the marriage, most couples learn they have little, or nothing, in common. They remain strangers, but try to make the most of it, each going his own way.

Further, there is the dominant sexist and undemocratic family environment which permeates marriage. These factors preclude any harmonious relationship. Egos abound, and the caretakers for the child have been, and are, generally speaking, a child-father and a child-mother who can only recycle ignorance.

Man, individually, should be able to look at man, collectively, and know that all prejudices, biases and ignorance are the products of the indifference to the child, an unrecognized homo sapien and the only conduit to an enlightened culture.

Hugo:

> "How much men are like the nettle!" After a short silence, he added: "My friends, remember this, that there are **no bad herbs, and no bad men; there are only bad cultivators.**" (emphasis added)
>
> —*Les Miserables,* p. 138.

A child is to any culture what seedlings are to a forest. Without seedlings, forests would vanish; without children mankind would soon disappear from the earth. Both must be nurtured to achieve full growth to their hereditary design; neither has a choice of either their genetic design or the environment in which they will be implanted.

For the seedling, the design and purpose of full growth is totally "physical"—nothing more, nothing less. Nature nurtures the forest seedling as it is simply a matter of the proper nutrients, i.e., water, light, chemicals, etc.

But this is not true for the child. For the child to be that which it was designed to be in the scheme of the universe, not only must the child achieve physical maturity, as the seedling, but it must, also, achieve **psychological maturity**. The *infant homo sapien* is born in a state of "ignorance and psychological immaturity." While Nature nurtures the forest seedling, the child must have a care-giver who not only must furnish the necessary nutrients to achieve physical maturity, but, also, an environment in which the child is encouraged to achieve emotional and psychological maturity. It is the responsibility of family (man/woman-the agent) to help the "infant" achieve enlightenment and psychological maturity, to become a rational individual—the biological inheritance. Every individual "being" must achieve both **physical** and **psychological maturity** to be a **homo sapien**.

> A GENUINE insight has a life of its own. "It dares appear and spread and glister in the World." Its strength is in its truth; and its sphere of influence is the total society in which men live together.
>
> One such insight—made clear to us by the scientists of human nature—**is that psychological maturing is something over and above physical maturing**. (emphasis added) It is itself a highly complex process of bringing our intellectual, emotional, and social selves up to the level of our bodily growth and environmental opportunities. **The achievement of such maturity is the greatest of our human triumphs**. (emphasis added)
>
> —*The Great Enterprize*, Preface, Overstreet.

It is man's **psychological existence** that separates him from the other organisms—that makes him unique—that gives him the capacity to be a "homo sapien"—the name is descriptive of the finished product, *rational*—the summit of man's existence.

The importance of the institution of marriage to society is such that society must fully appreciate how the relationship of the individual union of man/woman/child affects society. The family environment is not only important to the child, individually, but has a profound effect on the future of the culture of which the family is a part. The environment of which the child is a part is crucial to achieve an enlightened civilization. As children are taught, so the culture of which they are a part becomes, and the child learns, primarily, by **example**.

True, you have given a citizen to Rome;
And she shall thank you if the youth become
By your o'eruling care, or soon or late,
A useful member of the parent state.
For all depends on you: the stamp he'll take
From the strong impress which at first you make,
And prove, as vice or virtue was your aim,
His country's glory or his country's shame.
The stork with snakes or lizards, from the wood
And pathless wild, supports her callow brood;
And the fledged storklings, when to wing they take,
Seek the same reptiles through the devious brake.
The vulture snuffs from far the tainted gale,
And, hurrying where the putrid scents exhale,
From gibbets or dead dogs the carrion tears,
And to her young the loathsome dainty bears;
Her young, grown vigorous, hasten from the nest,
And gorge on corpses with the parent's zest
While Jove's own eagle, bird of noble blood,
Scours the wide champaign for untainted food,
As the swift hare or swifter fawn away,
And feeds her nestlings with the generous prey;
Her nestlings hence, when from the rock they spring
And, pinched by hunger, to the quarry wing,
Stoop only to the game they tasted first,
When clamorous from the shell to light they burst.

—*Satire XIV, Juvenal's Satires*

This was, also, noted by Joseph Joubert:

> Children have more need of models than of critics.
>
> —*Pense'es*

It is imperative for society to recognize that the hearth, the home (family), is not only the cornerstone on which an enlightened civilization must be built, but that the child is a homo sapien whose future is at risk.

To achieve this goal, Society's greatest energy must be employed for a radical transformation of the present social concepts of marriage, such to render impossible the repetition of the present horrors found therein, and make the hearth the cornerstone of enlightenment rather than the footstool for brutality, isolation, humiliation and exploitation. This is imperative if the sick body of the social organism is to be healed.

Since maturity is the state where the organism **is** that which it was **designed to be**, all energy, all effort, in all organisms, except man, is directed toward that goal: ACHIEVE MATURITY—COMPLETE THE DESIGN.

It is time for mankind to follow the lead of Nature.

While there has always been talk, talk, talk . . . no society, or culture, has stopped, looked at itself, and said, "No more. No longer will we recycle ignorance and immaturity. No more will there be war, violence, prejudice and hate."

There can be an enlightened culture. Enlighten the child and those things called "evil" will disappear from the culture. Man can achieve the design of his being—homo sapien.

It is time for America to make it a serious goal to achieve an enlightened culture, commit the necessary resources, and make the necessary sacrifices to achieve the goal, as the Russians and the Americans did to put a man in space and on the moon. This example for the World could help to eliminate war, violence, prejudice, hate.

First and foremost, every child birth out of wedlock fractures society. Society **must** return to the custom that made all pregnancies out of wedlock a No No, an event so embarrassing that the young girl was sent to visit an aunt in another town.

Next, a child cannot find the proper "models" in the teenage environment. You can only teach what you know. Every teenage child birth causes emotional distress and ruins lives too early. Every teenage child birth creates a handicap for many people, including the child.

A way to substantially reduce, and almost eliminate, teenage pregnancies is to separate boys and girls in school beginning with the fifth grade. I repeat for emphasis, not only would this substantially reduce, and almost eliminate, teenage pregnancies, but it is, also, beneficial in increasing grade scores in all subjects and reducing stress in the children. The indifference of society, presently, to child birth out of wedlock is a reflection of society's calloused indifference to children.

Rassellas observed:

> The good of the whole is the same with the good of all its parts.

Marriage (man/woman) is best for mankind since the husband and wife relationship is in accordance with nature, and the cell which makes the body of the social organism. Therefore, it must be best for individuals.

Since husband and wife are the cell which make the body of the social organism, this is where we must begin. Society must make the hearth the cornerstone of enlightenment. This will require radical transformation, an entirely new concept, of marriage from the very formation of the man/woman relationship for marriage through the advent of children.

Presently, and historically, the foundation of marriage is, and has been, ignorance and immaturity, with the rite of marriage being a narcissistic ritual devoid of reason and intelligence, which precluded establishing a satisfying and meaningful relationship.

This must change.

New occasions teach new duties; Time makes ancient good
uncouth;
They must upward still, and onward, who would keep abreast of
Truth;
Lo, before us gleam her camp-fires! we ourselves must Pilgrims
be,
Launch our Mayflower, and steer boldly through the desperate
winter sea,
Nor attempt the Future's portal with the Past's blood-rusted key.

—*Crisis*, Lowell

> You must empty out the dirty water before you fill the pitcher with clean.
>
> —*Suf. Humor.*

The "joining of hands" creates a "marriage" only if a meaningful relationship is established. A meaningful relationship is one that is free of any taint of coercion to maintain the relationship, either by fear, law or public opinion. It is absolutely necessary for the well being of the parties involved, and society as a whole, that the relationship be totally voluntary and that each enjoys the companionship of the other and views the other as equal. This environment stimulates sharing and growth; neither claim anything that is not freely conceded to the other; leading and following are reciprocal.

In a marriage with a "meaningful relationship," there would be a man and woman who, having achieved that maturity that recognizes the equality and self-dependance of all individuals, realize that complete fulfillment can only be achieved in the joining with one who has similarity of mind and sameness of purpose; then, walking together and sharing, help each other in the quest for full maturity.

In this relationship, the joining of hands creates a feeling of completeness—oneness—and life is felt as a blessing, a joy and fulfillment.

In such a relationship, the sexual impulse is excited by the "total" person and is only another way of sharing; it is recognized that the primary purpose of sexual activity is propagation.

Dr. G.C. Beale:

> In human beings, the physical union of real lovers becomes the vehicle and symbol of a spiritual union which cannot in any other way be so completely effected or expressed. From the bodily coalescence of lover and beloved, from the thrill and ecstasy kindled and rekindled in that close embrace, the full mutual surrender and uttermost delight in one another, there spring emotions and sympathies that are quite unattainable save in this manner.
>
> —*Wise Wedlock* (London [1922]), p. 57 sq.

Bertrand Russell observed that the sexual instinct:

> is not completely satisfied unless a man's whole being, mental quite as much physical, enters into the relation. . . . Love should be a tree whose roots are deep in the earth, but whose branches extend into heaven.
>
> —*Marriage and Morals*, (London, 1929), pp. 99, 224.

Procreation is then desired to share the blessing of life.

Not man alone, but all that roam the wood
Or wing the sky, or roll along the flood,
Each loves itself, but not itself alone,
Each sex desires alike, till two are one.
Nor ends the pleasure with the fierce embrace;
They love themselves, a third time, in their race.

—*Essay On Man*, Epistle III, l.119–124, Alexander Pope

Since this union is based on the premise that man is a rational being, that all are equal, that each must find his individuality and independence, that fulfillment is found in giving, these are the values that are transmitted to the progeny so that they, too, find joy in living.

A child is born; nor take the germ and make it
A bud of mortal beauty. Let the dews
Of knowledge, and the light of virtue wake it
In richest fragrance and in purest hues.

—Anonymous

How does a marriage result in a "meaningful relationship?"

The vital ingredient: CHOICE OF PARTNER!

One must conscientiously consider a possible partner's background, character, temperament, and maturity before matching with the same care as is done with physical considerations given horses, cattle and dogs in mating. The partners in a marriage should have basic similarity of taste, values, background, and both must have flexibility.

Mills believed:

> Intimate society between people radically dissimilar to one another, is an idle dream. Unlikeness may attract, but it is likeness which retains; and in proportion to the likeness is the suitability of the individuals to give each other a happy life.
>
> . . . when each of two persons, instead of being a nothing, is a something; when they are attached to one another, and are not too much unlike to begin with; the constant partaking in the same things, assisted by their sympathy, draws out the latent capacities of each for being interested in the things which were at first interesting only to the other; and works a gradual assimilation of the tastes and characters to one another, partly by the insensible modification of each, but more by a real enriching of the two natures,

> each acquiring the tastes and capacities of the other in addition to its own.
>
> —*The Subjection of Women.*

Before matching, it is imperative for each to "distinguish the real from the illusory, the long range from the temporary, the significant from the petty . . ." This can only be accomplished by instruction, intelligence and maturity. This is as vital for the full maturity of marriage, as light, air and nutrients are vital for full maturity of a seed. Then the rite of marriage will be a philosophical ritual devoid of narcissism.

Instruction should be a course of study that teaches all about the Institution of Marriage, and should begin no later than the sixth grade, and continue through high school. While this may seem like a long time, marriage is a complex institution and much is to be taught. Let us not forget that much studying is required for the professions—law, medicine, teaching, etc.—and marriage is the foundation of the culture. The curriculum for the course of study on the Institution of Marriage should include the personal aspects, legal aspects, social aspects, economic aspects and political aspects.

Such a program will take time to put into place. There are steps, however, society can take to immediately improve society.

Of instruction, intelligence and maturity, maturity is the most important for a meaningful relationship. As children cannot teach a "child" how to achieve psychological maturity, neither can children, generally speaking, form a relationship for marriage that is meaningful or one that can be expected to be lasting. Therefore, it is imperative for society to substantially raise the legal minimum age for marriage (as, also, for legal majority). While raising the age for marriage would not, alone, insure marriages to be lasting, it would be a major factor in reducing the number of divorces as it should almost eliminate those marriages formed on "romantic love."

Lord Beaconsfield wrote:

> All my friends who have married for love and beauty either beat their wives or live apart from them. This is literally the case. I may commit many follies in life, but I never intend to marry for "love," which I am sure is a guarantee of infelicity.
>
> —Quoted by A. Maurois, *Disraeli* (London, 1929), p. 67.

Furthermore, it would give the young time to experience the realities of life, know more of themselves and form some values, which would help in making the most important decision of their life. After all, education, in the most valid sense, is the process of maturation—growing up.

Bloch noted:

> It is a well-known fact that . . . marriages of reason are often more enduring than love marriages. This depends upon the nature of human love, which is by no means inalterable, but changes in accordance with the various developmental phases of the individual, needs new incitements and new individual relationships . . . All those who are well acquainted with humanity, all poets and psychologists, are in agreement respecting the fugitive character of youthful love. For this reason they advise against marriage concluded during the passion of early youth.
>
> —*The Sexual Life of Our Time* (London, 1908), p. 204.

Another additional requirement for marriage that would be very helpful is that after the parties (man/woman) have made application for a marriage license, there should be a mandatory waiting period of three months. During the three months waiting period the parties should be required to attend premarital counseling. The purpose of the counseling should be to help the parties to know and understand the relationship between marriage and society, purpose and goal of marriage, themselves, each other, that each will have to make adjustments, the complexities and intricacies of marriage and the duty and responsibility of a married couple to society.

While a mandatory waiting period of three months and premarital counseling are not now law, couples entering marriage would find it most useful and informative to voluntarily follow these steps.

And, it is essential that each tells the other anything that has happened in their life before marriage, that could, or would, affect the relationship after marriage.

Furthermore, people should learn that when they are seeking marriage and meet a person who appeals as a potential partner, a red flag should go up immediately. Now is the time for that person to look into the personality and character of the other person before getting involved emotionally.

After a child becomes part of the man/woman relationship, usually the parents, society must then walk the tightrope, delicately balancing the rights of the parents and their relationship with the child, and the rights of society in its interest to protect the child and bring forth an enlightened civilization. It is absolutely necessary that children become the primary concern of society. Months before the child is born, there should be mandatory parenting classes to instruct on what to expect when the child becomes part of the home, the total care of the child and the adjustments necessary to be made.

As the society becomes more enlightened—mature—the less need there will be for regulation concerning the child as this responsibility will be felt by the man and woman and the responsibility will be willingly accepted by the man and woman balancing their needs in their relationship with the child with society's needs in its relationship with the child. Each generation should build on the advancement of the preceding generation; ultimately, Society achieves enlightenment: a world in which there is no strife, no war, no violence, no competition, and very little government.

While Melville had the experience of observing numerous fully invested whales in their natural habitat to "truly and livingly" comprehend the nature of their being, the examples afforded mankind of "the fully invested homo sapien" to "truly and livingly" comprehend the nature of its being is sparse, but, we do have the description:

> What a piece of work is man! How noble in reason! How infinite in faculty! in form and moving how express and admirable! in action how like an angel! in apprehension how like a God! The beauty of the world! The paragon of animals! *Hamlet*, 1.252, Shakespeare.

Marriage can be, should be, the most satisfying of the personal relationships, the vehicle to love, joy, happiness and enlightenment. This relationship is described in the Apache Wedding Blessing:

> Now you will feel no rain, For each of you will be shelter to the other. Now you will feel no cold, For each of you will be warmth to the other. Now there is no more loneliness, For each of you will be companion to the other. Now you are two bodies, But there is only one life before you. Go now to your dwelling place To enter into the days of your togetherness. And may your days be good and long upon the earth.

The Institution of Marriage must be viewed as triadic, leading to:

1. Happiness and fulfillment for the parties;
2. Propagation of the race;
3. Enlightenment for mankind.

This could be reality.

This is human destiny.

Then let us pray that come it may
As come it will for a'[all] that,
That sense and worth, o'er a' the earth,
May bear the gree [win the prize], and a' that.
For a' that, and a' that,
It's coming yet, for a' that,
That man to man the warld o'er
Shall brothers be for a' that.
—*For A' That and A' That*, Robert Burns

And I saw a new heaven and a new
Earth: for the first heaven and the
First earth were passed away . . .
—*Revelation*, 21:1

Addendum

The saga of marriage is an effort to portray a marriage from the beginning to the end; hopefully, it may help someone who is struggling to end a marriage or give relief to someone who has just divorced.

The saga of marriage, as it is presented in the following chapters, is simplistic when viewed in light of reality. As I noted early in the book, it is impossible to portray the actual event of the disintegration of marriage as it is subtle and time consuming—an imperceptible erosion.

One can only give a few highlights. Even the parties, when questioned, can remember little more than a few highlights, since there is much suppression and rationalization, with feelings of guilt and fear.

The Saga—Two (2) as One (1)

A composite, with some repeating of material from previous chapters . . .

The husband and wife met at high school in their junior year. At the time of meeting, both were seventeen years old. They began dating soon after they met. Both of their parents worked in industry as hourly employees. Neither of their parents were college educated. When husband and wife met, each lived with their parents, each had a part-time job. The money made by each was used in whatever manner that was chosen; there was no required accountability to the parents as to how the money was spent. Neither husband or wife had ever "lived on their own." During the time of dating, the most serious conversation between husband and wife was which movie to see, where to eat or which clothes to buy. Of course, there was discussion of "cars." Husband and wife married within the year after graduating from high school.

Finding and providing for the furnishing of the living accommodations, planning meals, buying groceries, cooking and cleaning, arranging credit for various purchases, going to and coming from work, visiting and entertaining family and friends, sickness, buying clothes, paying bills, making decisions on priorities, choosing and selecting in an infinite number of ways begins. These activities are the realities of living. In these activities, the husband and wife find there are differences of opinion and arguing ensues. These activities, too, reveal the aspects of the other to each that were subconsciously overlooked, rationalized or concealed; in essence, each, gradually, learns and discovers the real person of the other—personality, maturity, disposition, intellectual capacity, character traits.

In the activities of living, they begin to know and learn each other in depth. Reality destroys the illusions, and brings forth, gradually, more differences of opinion and arguing, although the wife usually gives in to the husband.

As the luster of passion fades, as intimacy cools excitement, the chameleon changes colors, and the husband develops a dichotomous attitude toward the marriage. He enjoys his role as head of the family (power) and the convenience (satisfaction of the senses, i.e. sex, food, clothes washed and cleaned, etc.), but the responsibilities of marriage remain and they chafe! He does not feel the same relatedness to the wife as the wife toward him; for the husband, there is no fusion of identity with the wife. In fact, the husband's attitude toward his wife has strong similarities with his attitude toward his dog: in both relationships, he takes pride in looks, performance and obedience; in both relationships he believes he can take whatever liberties he desires; in both relationships he expects to be "master." The husband's concept of oneness is the same as "possession." The husband is annoyed by the restriction and responsibilities of marriage; he feels trapped; he blames it on the wife. He is resentful. The husband gradually changes from focusing his attention on the wife and the home to his job, hobbies, friends and, many, drinking (all of which are socially acceptable). The wife, who becomes more isolated, feels the change in the attitude of the husband toward her, and there are vocal expressions of such by her to him. Of course, there are denials by the husband, but, many times, there are temporary changes of behavior by the husband. More and more, the wife finds that she is doing most of the tasks at the home alone and is seeing less and less of the husband. As the evaporation of a heavy fog gradually reveals the landscape, time dispels the illusions of the marriage as envisioned—a panacea, a port; and the illusions of the "marriage love"—togetherness, a oneness. This leaves the wife distant in their relationship.

So, how do they recover a relationship that has grown cold?

A child, of course.

Upon receiving the news, the husband, initially, showed joy, joy, joy—a cultural tradition; the joy, in time, fades as did his passion for the wife.

Parenthetically, upon receiving the news, some husbands, initially, will show anger, verbally, by berating the wife for not having taken the proper precautions, and, some will become physically violent, even to the extent of hitting with their fist or kicking the wife in the stomach (the cases of Hilda and Jane but there are others of similar circumstances). Generally speaking, the husband will, in time, repress the anger and pretend that he is happy for the occasion—of course, these are the extremes.

Returning to the composite. . . .

After the arrival of the child, the life style changes. The wife no longer feels as alone, and the parties now have a toy, a plaything, a possession, a display, an exhibit, a spectacle, an exhibition and a show piece. Also, it is evidence to the wife that her husband loves her. The excitement of the arrival of the child is soon cooled by the needs and temperament of the child. The toy (child) must be cared for: fed, clothed, bathed, and it has a habit of making a lot of noise at various hours. Taking care of the child, generally speaking, will become the wife's responsibility.

The husband feels squeezed, financially, when food, clothes, diapers, medicine and various other items must be bought for the child. Within a short time, the child becomes a two-edged sword, pleasure, pride and responsibility, but more a sense of responsibility than pleasure and pride, especially for the wife. The husband's attitude of cooperation gradually fades, and, again, the wife finds that she is doing most of the tasks alone, and is seeing less and less of the husband. The husband is aware of the expectations of society: he is to provide a living for the family; the wife is to take care of the home and children. And "minimal" becomes his response to the marriage: minimal amount of "his" money and minimal amount of "his" time. Everything (time and money) above "minimal" is his to do with as he pleases; and, at times, things like rent, utilities, food, clothes, etc. must take second place to his "wants." Further, he believes that he is entitled to the earnings of the wife. And herein arises one of the thorns of the marriage: the wife believes that his "time," his "earnings," her "time," her "earnings" belong to the family, and there are many arguments. It is not unusual for the husband to leave the wife at home while he goes various places, but he prohibits her from going any place, including a visit to her family without his permission. For the husband, again, the home becomes a retreat from his job, outside activities and hobbies—a place of convenience, comfort and sustenance. In the cultural tradition, avoid and delegate become the husband's watchwords: avoid home and delegate to the wife all of the responsibilities of the home and marriage. The wife is expected to work, stay at home when she is not working, keep house, cook, attend to the children, be available for sex at his pleasure, pay the bills from her paycheck, allow him total freedom and the use of his money for his individual pleasure. A sense of divisiveness comes into the relationship, although the wife takes on the delegated responsibilities. Male domination arrives! Though resentful, wife accepts the roles of mother, maid and mistress to the husband to appease, and for harmony in the home for the children. The marriage settles into the rut of conventionality. This means husband does what he wishes and wife does what husband wishes.

The parties begin the pursuit of different interests: the man—politics, sports, hunting, fishing, fraternal organizations, etc.; the woman—cooking, sewing, church activities, home and children, etc. In effect, the husband and wife almost live separate lives, with minimal contact. "Separateness in marriage" has arrived.

Parenthetically "Separateness in marriage" is a myth, although it is, generally, practiced by society. The myth is that men and women have different interests that are gender based, a biological phenomenon. The myth arose from three factors: (1) most couples are incompatible in that their individual maturity, interests, temperament and, for many, even their goals in life, are totally different, or as Johnson observed, the couple is without "... conformity of opinions, similarity of manners, rectitude of judgment, or purity of sentiment"; (2) the marriage contract is considered to be indissoluble; and (3) the woman is not considered by the man to be able to discuss any topic but those concerning the home. "Separateness," under these circumstances, is a means of survival—the only way the parties can continue to live together. It is an accommodation for ignorance and fear, an effort to make the best of a hopeless situation.

"Separateness," too, is practiced in social gatherings—groups are made according to gender.

Returning to the saga ...

The marriage is now in the third year; the wife is working, although the husband uses her wages and exercises control over the money she has. Furthermore, the wife, for all practical purposes, is doing all housework, washing, cooking and taking care of the children—there are now two. The personal relationship between the husband and wife deteriorates; even though "love" is expressed by each for the other, it is the facade of "the marital relationship." Now, everything (work, household chores, paying bills, social activities, etc.) is done out of duty for "the marital relationship." Sex, for the wife, is not passion but an obligation. The "thrill" of the marriage is found in the "new": clothes, cars, home, furnishings, etc. The family is "doing things together" when they are watching the man's television programs, eating at a fast-food restaurant and taking an occasional outing or vacation.

The attitude of cooperation gradually fades. The woman learns the truth of Byron's observation that "love, to the man's life, is a thing apart ..." The woman feels the marriage vows were, effectively, a coronation ceremony for the man and sacrificial rites for her. This, too, is a cultural tradition!

In conformity with custom, so long as the husband continues

to tell the wife that he loves her, she continues her role of mother, maid and mistress. Essentially, the marriage is held together by the tenuous bond of "marriage." It is, simply, a living arrangement; a duality without synthesis. The wife is managing the husband's household. Two (2) as One (1) . . .

"There is an evil under the sun, and it is common among men."

Men and women marry and have not the power to enjoy the relationship but remain together and send forth a stinking savor.

It is an evil disease.

For Better or For Worse

The wife usually arrives home from work before the husband, and she begins to notice that on arriving home she has a sick, tight feeling in the pit of her stomach. She realizes that the husband would be home soon, and she was bracing herself for an onslaught of criticism: "The house is a mess—toys everywhere," "Why did you buy this—you don't need it," "You're not cooking like you did," and similar remarks. Further, when demands are made above what he considers to be the "minimal" (of which she had no knowledge as it changes with his moods), or when his authority is questioned, he lashes out. The wife and children are on the receiving end. There is almost constant argument over the buying of clothes and medical treatment, which things, sometimes, are denied even though needed.

In matters of discipline, the children face a "double whammy." When the children do something that irritates the husband, which is often, it is not unusual for the husband to ball up his fist, get right in the children's face shaking his fist, yelling at the top of his voice threats of what he will do to them, or to jerk them up and hit or shake them. And with the wife, it is either the screaming at the children such things as "I hate you"; "You are stupid"; "I wish you had never been born," or it may be a hit, jerk, slap or spanking.

In addition to criticizing the wife at home, the husband has begun "putting her down," and "humiliating her" in public gatherings—with their friends, at parties, but especially with her family and her colleagues at work. It does not go unnoticed as many of her friends comment on the way "he treats her." When the wife speaks to the husband about the matter, his reply is either: You're too sensitive—everybody else laughed; You're making a big deal out of nothing; I'm sorry—I'll do better.

But, soon, it all begins again. And, it is not too long before the husband begins to point out other women to the wife, comment on their attributes (the ones he thought she didn't have), and make remarks like, "She can eat crackers in my bed anytime," etc.

Sometimes the husband would come home and say, "Let's go out to eat—choose where you want to go." Then, as the wife was preparing for the occasion, the husband would say, suddenly, "No, I've changed my mind—we have some spaghetti in the refrigerator that we need to fix." Similar incidents happened so many times that the wife would no longer have expectations of eating out.

For the wife, the marriage is a commitment; she struggles to keep it intact. She rationalizes that all marriages have "their ups and downs." But, over and over and over again, the wife tries to talk with the husband about the marriage—to no avail. His feelings are that the wife is "blaming" him, that she wants him to be "perfect," or that he ". . . just cannot talk to her." Everything is fine as far as he is concerned; he cannot understand her discontent. The wife clings to the hope that the husband will soon be the way he used to be in their early relationship. Yet, even under these circumstances, there is an occasional moment of joy. The wife doubles her effort to keep the home life as happy and free of stress as possible, including another talk with the children. The relationship between the husband and wife is superficial. Both would say they love the other and everything is O.K., but that it would be great if the other would only change and do so and so.

As time goes by, when the wife tries to talk about the marriage, the husband begins to tell her that she can leave the home anytime, and he would be glad if she did—in front of the children. And, then, it is not too very long before he begins to threaten to leave the home permanently, in front of the children. Eventually, the husband begins to leave the home for several days at a time without telling the wife and children where he is. Sometimes, on his return, the husband hints that he might have been with another woman, in front of the children.

The wife begins to feel very much alone with the pressure of bearing most responsibilities: financial, discipline of children, decisions of household, etc., and while she has experienced emotional uncertainty, slavery and servitude (effectively), neglect and aloneness, she remains in the marriage.

And, then, during an argument one day the husband calls the wife "you dumb bitch," in front of the children; soon thereafter in another argument, it's "you mean, vicious, silly ass,"—in front of the children; thereafter, it is constant and more vicious: "you slut . . . whore . . . ignoramus"—in front of the children.

Verbal abuse begins . . . and the wife remains in the marriage.

The wife attributes the verbal abuse by the husband to anger without malicious intent even though the abuse "cuts her to the quick." But, the relationship between the wife and husband is altered as there now is a certain subconscious tension felt by the wife.

Some time thereafter, the **verbal abuse** turns to **threats of physical abuse**.

It is a Saturday night and the husband has been drinking beer all day. An argument develops in front of the children while they are in the kitchen, and the husband, suddenly, grabs a knife, holds it at the wife's throat, and threatens to cut it ". . . if the bitch don't shut up."

On another occasion when the husband had been drinking beer all day, the family is eating the evening meal, and the wife, not too long thereafter, says something that throws the husband into a "fit of anger." He begins yelling obscenities at the wife and leaves the room; the children begin sobbing and crying "Daddy don't hurt mummy." Immediately the husband returns holding a pistol with the trigger cocked and puts it to her head and threatens to kill or maim her ". . . if that happens again."

Again, the wife attributes the "threats of harm" by the husband to "anger" even though she is now fearful of physical harm. And while the wife is now very guarded in her conversations with the husband, and tension increases between them, the wife remains in the marriage.

Then, the wife's fear of physical harm happens.

It is Saturday night and the family has just returned to the home from eating pizza. The husband has been drinking beer since late morning; he had purchased a 24-pack on Friday night. The family begins watching a movie that was rented. Soon after starting to watch the movie, an argument develops between the husband and wife, and, suddenly, the husband turns to the wife, who is sitting in a chair beside him, and slaps her in the mouth, telling her ". . . don't argue with me." The wife is stunned and does not feel the blood trickling down her lip. The children, too, are shocked and, when they see the blood on their mummy, begin to cry. The husband tells the wife to go wash her face; she obeys. The wife and children then go to bed.

The next morning the husband apologizes to the wife and children. He tells the wife that he loves her, and that he had just lost his temper. The wife accepts the husband's apology, but she enters a state of confusion, fear and loneliness. She is caught between her intellect and emotions. It is hard for her to accept that someone who loves her would hurt her. The wife rationalizes that she did something to provoke the abuse, accepts the blame.

It happens again. The circumstances are very similar. The husband has been drinking beer all day, preparations are being made to eat the evening meal, the family is in the kitchen, the wife says something and, suddenly, the husband hits the wife with his fist on the eye and knocks her to the floor. The next morning, the wife has a black eye. Again, the husband apologizes to the wife and children. He tells the wife that he loves her, and that he did not know what he was doing since he had been drinking. Again, the wife accepts the husband's apology, and, again, rationalizes that she did something to provoke the abuse, accepts the blame.

And, then, there are more occasions of physical abuse—cuts, bruises, a broken tooth, twisted arms—again, again, and again.

After each abuse, the wife accepts the husband's apology, affirmation of love and excuse that he had just lost his temper, or that he really didn't know what he was doing since he was drinking and rationalizes that she did something to provoke the abuse, accepts the blame.

The wife remains in the marriage.

Over and over and over again, the wife tries to talk with the husband about the marriage—to no avail. Everything is fine as far as he is concerned; he cannot understand her discontent.

Nor does she get any consolation, after she has overcome her embarrassment to speak of it, from family or friends. From these encounters with society, the wife learns that, in the arena of marriage, the rules and concepts totally favor the man—psychologically and practically. The man finds social acceptance for just about anything he wants to do. She feels resentment in her social status as His helpmate . . . who is to abide by his wishes, whims, beliefs; to be physically chastised (beaten) when she exerts her independence, disagrees with him, fails to foresee his mood, irritates him or if he needs a punching bag. He is to be pampered and praised, fed when hungry, satisfied sexually by any method that suits his fancy at the given moment. The wife should work, pay the bills, keep the house, cook the meals, raise the children (even though she is inferior), stay interested in his hobbies, demand as little money from him as possible (his money is needed for his hobbies and pleasures), and keep the home fires burning.

It becomes apparent to the wife:

> Immodest creature, you do not want a woman who will accept your faults, you want one who pretends that you are faultless—one who will caress the hand that strikes her and kiss the lips that lie to her.
>
> —*The Intimate Journal of George Sand*, (1834)

The wife doubles her effort to keep the home life happy, free of stress as possible, including another talk with the children. She, now, tries to third guess the husband's moods. She even tries to be more aggressive sexually even though she is without desire; she continues to cater to his whims.

"Love," for the wife, becomes an orgasm, security, habit, someone to take care of her, avoidance, children, a long marriage, a religious belief or the reluctance to admit one should not have married.

What the wife feels as "love" is really "fear" rationalized. There are many fears: fear of being unable to make it by herself, fear of being alone, fear of criticism, fear of loneliness, fear of failure, fear of rejection, etc. All is rationalized.

The union continues, frequency becomes habit, habit license, license necessity, necessity, "the" marriage. She clings to the hope that he will soon be the way he used to be.

But, such is not to be.

It is summertime; the children are visiting with the grandparents. It is Tuesday; the wife tells the story in her affidavit to the authorities:

> I arrived home from work about 6:10 p.m. on Tuesday, August 1, 1983. Jim was laying on the couch drunk and passed out. I changed clothes, emptied the trash, picked up around the house, trying to be as quiet as I could. I did not want to awaken Jim because I knew how mean he could get when he was drinking. Jim woke about 6:40 p.m. He said, what are we having for supper? I said spaghetti—that's about all we have. I warmed the spaghetti in the microwave, fixed our plates and carried them in the living room. He was in his chair, I got on the sofa. Jim finished eating. He said, I want to talk to you.
>
> He came over to the sofa and sat beside me. He asked me where my money was. I said Jim, I don't have but a few dollars, today is not payday, this is Tuesday not Thursday. He started slapping me about the face, saying: "Your money is my money, do you

hear me?" I remember falling on the floor, he got on top of me and started beating me about the face again. He would hit me over and over. He grabbed me by my hair and started beating my head against the floor. Each time my head hit the floor, I would see stars. I put my right hand to the back of my head to cushion the blows, but he said you bitch, move your hand or I'll kill you. I'll fix your face where nobody will ever want to look at you. He put his knee across my neck, grabbed me by the hair and pull my head toward his knee so he could choke me. I think I may have blacked out. I thought I was dying.

He started toward the bedroom. I went to the front door. I had my hand on the door knob when Jim got to me. He grabbed me by my hair and started beating my head against the door, saying I had better not try to leave again. He tore my sweater and bra off me. He jerked my shorts off, my panties tore. He beat me about the face, head and started choking me again. It felt like he was breaking my neck. I must have blacked out again. I remember being in the middle of the floor with Jim beating me about the face. The pain was unbearable, I was so sick. I couldn't stand up anymore. He would slap me across the face, I would fall to the floor, he would make me get up so he could slap me again. He would say: "Stand up or I'll kill you." I would say, "please don't hit me anymore. Please don't hurt me anymore." He would hit me that much harder.

At this point, I could not stand the pain anymore. I begged God to just go ahead and let me die. He pulled me into the bathroom with him. He used the bathroom. He let me wet a wash cloth with cold water to put on my face. We went to the bedroom and got on the bed. He said I wasn't going to work in the morning. I was to say that I fell out the door. He said I had better not tell anybody what he did to me. My nose and throat filled with blood. I was trying to breathe and blew a blood clot out of my nose, it fell on Jim's knee. It made Jim mad. He made me get a tissue and clean the blood off his knee. I was hurting so bad, I could barely move my head. I was sick and throwing up. I begged Jim to call his mother to come help me. He said no. I begged him to carry me to the hospital or just get somebody to help me. He said no that he would help me. I remember my Mother saying she prayed for my safety every night. She prayed that if Jim raised his hand to hit me that God would paralyze his arm. I started praying, Jesus remember my mother's prayer. Please don't let me die. I prayed this over and over. God, please don't let me die. I won't ever come back to Jim again.

I prayed for a long time. I could tell by Jim's breathing that he was passed out. I prayed, God, please help me get away. Give me the strength to get up. I managed to raise up on the side of the bed. I picked up my house robe off the chair beside my bed. I stood up, my head was spinning around and around. I was dizzy, I kept going sideways. I had lost all my balance. I would try and make it to the bathroom and if he heard me, I would say I had to use the bathroom. I could still hear his heavy breathing. I kept praying, God, please give me the strength to get away from here. Please don't let me die.

I got to the back door, eased it open and slipped outside. I gently closed the door. This is where God picked me up and carried me barefoot. I climbed over a wire fence with barbed wires across the top. The barbed wire stuck in my hands and fingers. I headed toward a house with lights on. I banged on their back door. A man came to the door. I said please let me in, my husband has beat me and tried to kill me. Please call the County and an ambulance. He let me in, I collapsed on their floor. I thanked God for letting me get away alive. Please don't let me die, God. I lay there praying and was hurting and too sick to move. I love you Jesus.

The County Deputies came and I was taken to the hospital by ambulance.

History and Physical

This twenty-eight-year-old white female was in previously good health, was beaten up by her husband last night over a period of about two hours in which he repeatedly hit her head and face against the wall and floor. When he went to sleep the patient snuck out and was brought to the ER via EMS.

ASSESSMENT:

1. Possible skull fracture.
2. Head trauma.
3. Possible sinusitis.
4. Vertigo secondary to inner ear disturbance from trauma.
5. Wife abuse.

Divorce—The Challenge

While the wife was in the hospital, the husband apologized to her, as in the past, with the excuse that he really didn't know what he was doing since he was drinking, and, again, there was an affirmation of love. But, this time, from the wife, there was only silence.

This incident had given the wife time for reflection, a time to think. She did not like what she now knew to be true: that her husband severely injured her, that her husband did not really care for her as a person, that he had been using her (i.e. sex, household chores, taking care of children, taking money she earned), that he was not going to change, that things would remain as they are, or get worse. Acknowledging that the marriage was over, all dreams and plans were shattered, all hope gone—was a bitter pill to swallow. The wife found she was suddenly in a state of "psychic shock," although she did not know it. Psychic shock is to the mind what physical shock is to the body. It is a state of extreme mental confusion. It is brought on by a sense of disorganization, displacement, aloneness, fear, isolation and confrontation. The end result is TRAUMA! CRISIS! If the force of this "shock" could be measured, as is the "shock-force" of an earthquake, it would exceed the capacity of the Richter Scale.

Upon returning home after three days in the hospital, the wife is still in a state of shock, physical and mental, and is as a zombie. Upon resuming her daily routine (work, taking care of the children and house), everything she does is rote, from habit. The husband is away from home more than usual. There is very little conversation within the family. The children, who were with her parents during her stay in the hospital, sense something is different, but do not ask any questions.

While the husband and wife are still sharing the same bed, there is no sex; the wife makes excuses. She keeps her distance from the husband, and has as little conversation as possible with him. Within the second month after her return from the hospital, the husband begins to express his displeasure about having no sex. It begins to be almost a nightly routine. Then, he begins to threaten to go outside of the marriage for sex. One night after threatening to go outside of the marriage, the wife says, "Fine. It is O.K. with me." The husband gets mad, reminds her of her wifely duty, grabs her arms, and tries to force himself on her; the wife screams, the husband releases her. The children appear at the bedroom door. The wife leaves the bedroom, goes and sleeps with the girl. This becomes the sleeping arrangement.

The wife now makes an effort to talk with the husband about ending the marriage, directly and indirectly, as she had tried to talk with him about their relationship earlier, directly and indirectly. Now, as then, he does not listen. He does not understand what she is talking about; for him, everything is fine. The husband says that he will give the wife time to recover her senses. The family, now, very seldom sees the husband as they have usually gone to bed when he comes home.

The stage is set; the issues joined. If the marriage is to be ended, she will have to do it, alone—as she carried the marriage. She contends with a feeling of guilt in breaking the marriage, even though she has done everything possible to save it. She cares for her husband in the sense that she does not want to hurt him, but not the kind of caring that makes a marriage.

She knows she can take no more; that, while she would have it differently, she can no longer respond to the man emotionally. She feels a bewilderment of habit, love, commitment and many fears: being alone, criticism, failure, rejection, physical harm and loneliness. She cries enough tears to float a boat, but she cannot continue the marriage. In her despondency, there are times when she feels she is "going crazy," even thinks of suicide, believing that death would be the best way out—hers or his.

Sometime after the incident of the husband trying to force sex, the wife, while at work, calls a friend, who had gone through a divorce, and, discreetly, found out the lawyer who represented her. She wrote his name down and found his office number, which she wrote under his name. She immediately started dialing the number when, suddenly, the question occurred to her, "What will my family and friends think when I tell them I am getting a divorce?" She hung up the phone. She folded the paper on which she had written the name and number of the lawyer, and placed it in her purse in a discreet place. The matter remained in the back of her mind. Several days later, at night, after the children had gone to bed, and the husband was not in the house, she called her friend again, and moved the conversation in the direction of the friend's divorce, and, specifically, what her family and friends thought about the divorce. She learns from her friend that it is impossible to know what they will think until it happens. Some may think it was her fault, or that she did not try hard enough, or that she should have stayed in the marriage because of the children, but that most will simply accept it. After ending the conversation, she does not feel any relief, only isolation, emotional anxiety and frustration. She had a writing pad and pencil in her hand, thinking she may need to make some notes. Suddenly, she found herself writing. . . .

All is well again
I think I'm finally getting over you.
We started out such good friends
We had everyone fooled
They thought our love would never end
Our love has long since cooled.
You always treated me so kind
Your loving actions made me so sure
But you've changed and it rocks my mind

And you don't even bring me flowers anymore.
So now it's over, I will not fret
The healing won't start unless I learn to forget.

—Anonymous

She laid the writing pad and pencil on the bedside table, and turned out the light.

During the next few weeks, she makes appointments with the lawyer, but, as the hour approaches, she calls and cancels as she feels a doubt as to whether she is doing the right thing—a doubt brought on by fear of whether she can make it on her own, loneliness, and criticism. She soon discovers that it takes more "guts" to walk into a lawyer's office to get a divorce than it did to walk down the aisle to get married, that getting a divorce is easier said than done. And it is just beginning. She has a morbid fear of being unable to make it on her own, she knows she must make the effort to find the harmony, peace and meaning that has been denied in the relationship. The crisis has arrived, she knows. With the relationship as it is between her and the husband, she knows she must proceed with the divorce, or she will never do it.

She learns:

". . . nothing has more strength than dire necessity."

—Euripides

She remembers a passage from Shakespeare:

There is a tide in the affairs of men,
Which, taken at the flood, leads on to fortune;
Omitted, all the voyage of their life
Is bound in shallows and in miseries;

She "takes the current when it serves . . ." and makes another appointment. On the day of the appointment, with much apprehension, and recognizing that "necessity is above the Gods themselves," she keeps the appointment. Advice is given, and arrangements are made for the divorce. As she leaves the lawyer's office, she feels as though a great weight had been lifted from her shoulders.

> I know that I am a slave and you are my lord. The law of this country has made you my master. You can bind my body, tie my hands, govern my actions: you are the strongest, and society adds to your power; but with my will, sir, you can do nothing.
>
> —*Indiana*, Preface, George Sand

But even as she was seeking advice concerning the legal aspects of divorce, etc., her emotions are seeking a way to preserve the status quo, being in a state of anxiety, frustration and confusion.

She says nothing to her husband about seeing a lawyer, not knowing how he would respond. Soon after the appointment with the lawyer, the papers for the divorce on the grounds of habitual drunkenness and physical cruelty, with a Restraining Order, are served on the husband. After reading the papers, the husband goes into a rage, telling the wife how sorry she will be for doing this, cursing and calling her the worst names he can think of, and threatens her with all kinds of retaliations, including getting custody of the children, and physical abuse—all while the children were present. But the husband does not bother the wife physically. Taking his clothes, and telling the wife he would be back for his other personal things later, the husband leaves the house the next day. That night the wife and children felt a peace and tranquillity that had not been experienced in years.

The husband employs a lawyer to contest the divorce. During the entire time while waiting for the final hearing, the husband creates much tension; either he is making threats to the wife as to what the Court is going to do to her, or, on most of the visitations with the children, he makes a scene.

On the week before the final hearing is scheduled, the wife is informed by her lawyer that there will not be a contested hearing—the husband has agreed to her terms for the divorce.

On reflection, the wife recognizes that this was the husband's character—a big bluff—and remembers another passage from Shakespeare, which she quotes aloud:

Hollow men, like horses hot at hand,
Make gallant show and promise of their mettle;
But when they should endure the bloody spur,
They fall their crests, and, like deceitful jades,
Sink in the trial.

But the wife is glad that the divorce had been resolved. She had been dreading the hearing.

The wife is in a relaxed mood on her way to the final hearing . . .

> What I'm doing in this car flying down these screaming highways is getting my tail to Juarez so I can legally rid myself of the crummy son-of-a-bitch who promised me a tomorrow like a yummy fruitcake and delivered instead wilted lettuce, rotted cucumber and a garbage of life.
>
> —*Long Division*, Anne Richardson Roiphe, 1972.

After the hearing was over, on her way home, the wife was reflecting on the past events, and she realized that

Fear is a liar, poisoning today
With fantasies of what may come tomorrow,
Until each joy is shadowed by a sorrow,
And dreading it, we leak our lives away.

—Anonymous

for, if it had not been for "fear," she would have obtained the divorce a long time ago. The task has taken the strength of Samson, the patience of Job, the finesse of Solomon. Marriage, for her, began with "desire" without "love" and ended in "love" without "desire."

From darkness and death, love is born; then order and beauty.

Upon reflection, she realized that the divorce was to her self-reliance that the marriage was to her dependency; to the confrontation that the marriage was to escape, and to reality that the marriage was to illusion.

It was now over, but

> Mary. Well being divorced is like being hit by a mack truck. If you live through it, you start looking very carefully to the right and to the left.
>
> —*Mary, Mary*, Act I, Jean Kerr, 1960.

Yet, she knew that it was her efforts that freed the parties from a malignant, "dead" relationship, and from the ashes of this "dead" relationship, the parties, as the Phoenix, had the chance of finding a live, more vital relationship. It is a new beginning—with experience! She felt good!

So endeth this Saga.

The Aspects of Divorce

The ceremony for marriage and the legal procedure for divorce are rites of passage, as is a funeral, and are for the parties involved and society. The ceremonies (marriage, divorce and funeral) are efforts to make tangible the intangible. They are signals of a "beginning," and an "end," a "closing" and an "opening."

A "marriage" is the "bond" between the man and woman; it is not the vows. The bond between the man and woman was formed before the vows, and the ceremony simply confirms that bond to society.

A divorce is not the act that ends a marriage (bond between the man and woman) as many people think. The intimate-personal relationship (the bond) between the man and woman ended before the "legal" event; the divorce confirms that rupture, as death has occurred before the funeral rites. It is the tangible signal to the parties and the world that a previous intimate-personal relationship has ended: a procedure that permits the pursuit of a new life. It is the legal "form" one must go thru to end the "legal relationship," so the parties are free to enter into another intimate-personal relationship with someone else. Simply, it confirms that which was known.

Divorce is generally thought of as a "legal" event only, even within the legal profession. But, it is more.

Divorce has a different effect, generally speaking, on men and women.

Men, generally, place more importance on the habits and the routine of marriage. Deprived of the habits and routine of the marriage, the man feels a loneliness that he confuses with "love." Therefore, they are willing, generally, to continue marriage even though there is, and has been, discord in the marriage. However, if forced from the habits and the routine of marriage long enough, they will not desire to continue the marriage, and will say that "love" for the woman was lost.

Divorce for the man is, mostly, a matter of inconvenience, and it may, or may not, have a mild traumatic effect. It is primarily disorganization.

But, generally speaking, divorce means "woman," and getting a divorce is not simple, as many people think, especially for the woman.

The initial purpose of the work was to put together a manual that could benefit the woman by helping her to identify her feeling during this emotional upheaval, to be a "friend" as she walked through the "valley of the shadow of death," something that would help her to keep the faith that the sun would shine again.

Why is a divorce not simple?

Divorce, for the woman, is a "traumatic emotional event!" It is a violent encounter—a collision, psychologically. The woman must, first, acknowledge that her man does not love her, and, second, accept the fact that all of her hopes and dreams are shattered, and the reality that they will not, cannot, be, with the resulting necessity of the withdrawal and separation of identity with the man. Before the woman can leave the man, she must obliterate the identity with him and sever the "umbilical connection," and this leaves her alone, psychologically!

This is traumatic!

The obliteration of identity with the man, the crushing of all the hopes and dreams of the marriage, feeling alone, and the direct confrontation of societal and religious views of marriage results in "**psychic shock**!" This is as severe to the psyche as severe injuries are to the body.

Fromm pointed out:

> To feel completely alone and isolated leads to mental disintegration just as physical starvation leads to death . . . The kind of relatedness to the world may be noble or trivial, but even being related to the basest kind of pattern is immensely preferable to being alone. Religion and nationalism, as well as any custom and any belief however absurd and degrading, if it only connects the individual with others, are refuges from what man most dreads: isolation.
>
> —*Escape From Freedom*, op. cit., 34, 35.

In this state of anxiety, the woman feels fear without knowing of what; guilt without knowing why; aloneness without knowing how, and loss of hope.

Hesse:

> It is always difficult to be born. You know the chick does not find it easy to break his way out of the shell.
>
> —*Demian*

In fact, the "ending" of the relationship creates for many women such emotional confusion that many believe they "are going crazy," or that death would be the easy way out. Some attempt suicide. Consequently, the decision to get a divorce is one that has been arrived at after a methodical trial and error evaluation, or analysis—mentally and emotionally. Regardless of the conditions under which she is living, generally speaking, a woman has to prepare psychologically for a divorce as one prepares physically to climb Mt. Everest. The greater the felt need by the woman for the marriage as a panacea, the more difficult it is to ultimately dissolve the union. Many women try for a divorce but fail emotionally (psychologically)—". . . when they should endure the bloody spur, they fail their crests, and . . . sink in the trial."

It is not unusual for a woman to make more than one appointment, and cancel out before finally keeping the appointment, or to relate in the interview that she had ridden by the office several times before making the appointment, and keeping the appointment does not mean she will complete the divorce—even if she pays a retainer fee.

Some examples (the names are changed):

Helen. When I first met Helen she was twenty-three years old, a blonde, physically attractive high school graduate, worked in an industrial plant, very sharp mentally, had been married approximately four years, had two children. Her husband was two years older, worked in the same plant, had spent a couple of years in service, completed his GED while in service. She was seeking a divorce because her husband drank excessively, and, when he was drinking, he would physically and verbally abused her. The physical abuse, at this point, was mostly slapping; the verbal abuse was threatening to do more serious bodily harm and calling her names, i.e. slut, stupid, etc. A retainer fee was paid, a divorce action was begun but there was reconciliation. A divorce action was begun with reconciliation a couple of times over the next few years. The husband's drinking and abuse spiraled. Finally, twelve years after first seeing her, and now with five children, the divorce was completed.

Delores. Delores was thirty years old when she came for a divorce. She had been married fifteen years, had three children with the oldest being thirteen years old—a girl. She had dropped out of high school after marriage and was working in an industrial plant. Early in the marriage, she began to find beer cans and bottles in the utility room, the closets and the kitchen cabinets. He became a stranger to the family early on. After much verbal abuse, serious threats of physical abuse and several reconciliations, the divorce was completed four years later.

Faye. When I first met Faye, she was twenty-four years old, had been married for five years, and had two children. Her husband was two years older, and both worked in an industrial plant. They married very soon after graduating from high school. Within a year after marriage, he began drinking excessively, physically abusing her, leaving bruises on her arms, face and legs, and verbally abusing her with such names as slut, whore and others. On one occasion, he left and was gone for three months without her knowing where he was. A divorce action was begun; reconciliation. Six years later the divorce was completed; his conduct had grown worse during the years.

An occurrence:

> Karen Nittle was a career woman, divorcee and a mother when she met the man who was to become her second husband.
>
> She met him at a church function, and they dated almost every day for eight months. They had daily devotionals together and attended the same Bible class.
>
> "He . . . was a very religious person," said Mrs. Nittle, a Spartanburg native who spoke during a recent domestic violence seminar at Tri-County TEC.
>
> That is how she entered the marriage with him—with thoughts that she had found a man who cared deeply about her and her beliefs as a Christian.
>
> No one would have thought that within a year she would be the victim of spouse abuse, she said.
>
> Six months into the marriage, she became pregnant. That is when the trouble began, she said at the seminar.
>
> Though she and her husband decided to have a child of their own, Mrs. Nittle said he changed his mind—he didn't want a child after all. He began pressuring her to have an abortion, she said. She refused.
>
> Throughout the pregnancy she suffered constant verbal abuse from her husband, she claimed. He compared her to other women in an effort to reveal her shortcomings and faults, she said. He called her son degrading names, she said.
>
> "Verbal abuse is 10 times worse than physical abuse," said the attractive slender 40-year-old in a calm, controlled voice. "Bones heal. The emotional scars take a long time."
>
> Though the public sometimes has the impression that abused wives provoke their husband's rage, "That's not so," Mrs. Nittle

said. "A person is not going to deliberately set fire to something that is going to explode in their faces."

For that reason, she and her son tried to make home life as happy and free of stress, as possible. Nevertheless, she said her husband was always angry.

Four days after her second child, also a son, was born, he began to physically abuse her, she alleged. At times, she was beaten, slapped and knocked to the floor, she said. She suffered broken ribs, and a blow to the left cheek left one-quarter of her face paralyzed, she said.

Despite the abuse, Mrs. Nittle said it was hard for her to leave. She and her husband, a Canadian citizen, had moved to Canada from the Pacific Northwest. It was difficult for her to pack up and leave a country—and a man—she loved.

"I loved him. I still love him," she said quietly. "He had tremendous qualities as a person, as a man."

And she was emotionally dependent on him. She said she still harbored guilt feelings that her first marriage had failed—she wanted this one to succeed.

"When a person stays in a situation like I did, it's not that they like it, " she explained. "It's just that it is hard to leave . . . hard to accept that someone who loves you, who has said they love you . . . would hurt you."

Finally Feb. 14, Valentine's Day, three years ago, she decided to leave. She said she was afraid her husband's influence on her children would cause them to become batterers themselves. Already her baby—whom her husband would hold in one arm as he abused her—was showing signs of aggression, she said.

—*Anderson Independent-Mail*, Sun., Oct. 7, 1984, 1B

Hopefully, these examples can give an understanding of how difficult it is to end a marriage for the woman.

For the woman, divorce is displacement, isolation, confrontation, and disorganization.

Displacement is the most difficult. It is her need to psychologically withdraw her merger with the man from the man—her commitment. This, essentially, gives her a feeling of being alone in the world.

Isolation happens when she suddenly realizes that she, now, must make all decisions on her own without the help of the man. Further, she is shunned by many of her social peers. A woman who is separated from her husband creates a sense of guilt in many of her female acquaintances who feel they should do the same thing but cannot find the courage and shun her. Also, a woman who is separated from her husband is felt a threat, socially, by many women to their own marriage and shun her.

Confrontation is the second most difficult. She is confronted with the realization that all of her hopes and dreams for the marriage are gone; this creates a psychological void. More, there are still some segments of society who believe divorce is still taboo—"You made your bed, now lie in it"—creating the ultimate guilt trip. Further, there was her own expectation that the marriage was "until death," which is compounded by the religious exhortation "What God has put together, let no man put asunder."

Disorganization happens when her everyday habits of the marriage change, as they must. There is a certain disorganization felt that has a disruptive effect which in turn creates a certain feeling of loneliness.

For the woman, all of these create emotional trauma—in all its ramifications—that the woman will never feel again. The woman, in this emotional trauma, goes through stages to finally "get" a divorce. The stages fall into a pattern:

1. Self-reproach—blames herself for the deteriorating relationship in the marriage. Many times she blames the deteriorating relationship in the marriage on the reason for the marriage.
2. Trial & Error—does various things to appease husband.
3. Try & Try & Try Again—rationalizes to save relationship. Believes things will get better.

4. Shock—admits marriage is over and cannot continue the relationship.
5. Grief—dispels all illusions—abandons all dreams she had for the marriage.
6. Divorce.
7. Recovery—man is no longer any part of her life, and dreams of marriage are totally reconciled. She feels a harmony with herself and wonders why she took so long to get the divorce.

Why does the woman continue in such a relationship? There are many reasons:

1. Fear of not being able to survive alone emotionally and physically. This is a fear of many, many women;
2. Fear of social criticism—feels she is expected to remain regardless;
3. Fear of violation of religious admonition: "What God has joined together, let no man put asunder."
4. Fear of failure;
5. Fear of being injured by man if she leaves;
6. Confusion of love—rationalization based on fears;
7. The "habit of marriage."

Divorce for the woman is, generally speaking, an effort to find harmony, peace and meaning in life after coming to an understanding of the "pseudomorphis" (false formation), which the marriage was—a recognition that the union began with "the seed of rot"—which may be one or more of: married too young, wanted to get away from home, pregnant, didn't know what I was doing, thought we were in love, wanted a home or thought I knew what I was doing.

It is society's failure to acknowledge that the relationship of the parties is the essential element of marriage that is, and has been, responsible for millions living abjectly, suffering all the pains of hell. "Mayhem in the families" is no respecter of person, faith or nationality. As most people do not want to be kept alive on a machine when all their vital functions are gone, neither should a couple remain together after the bond has dissolved that made the marriage. Those who advocate that a couple should remain together for the sake of the children even after their personal relationship has ruptured do not care for children.

Society's negative attitude about divorce has been as repressive to many married couples, and especially the women, as any totalitarian authority, and is as outdated as is the concept of "bleeding" to cure illness. This negative attitude, for the most part, arose from organized religion, in its quest for power, and has been rubber-stamped by politicians. The religious concepts are devoid of any understanding of the essential element of a marriage, and make "form" (the vows) more important than "substance" (the relationship of the parties). The story of the Marriage Institution has confirmed the proverb:

> He who will not learn from the past is destined to repeat it.

There is no advantage to society to "save" a relationship (marriage) that is malignant, and these concepts (negative attitude and religious concepts) have the same merit that Hume felt about a book that contains nothing of substance:

> If we take in our hand any volume . . . let us ask, "Does it contain any experimental reasoning concerning matter of fact and existence?" No. Commit it then to the flames for it can contain nothing but sophistry and illusion.

No words can better describe these concepts than "sophistry and illusion." Furthermore, these same concepts have been a significant obstacle in society's effort to achieve an enlightened culture. No society that is rigid in its beliefs can achieve enlightenment.

William James gave the following advice to keep the mind alive and resilient: (1) see an alternative; (2) do not take the usual for granted; (3) refuse to make conventionalities fluid again except in dire necessity; (4) imagine foreign states of mind.

Advice for an individual is, also, valid for a society.

Parenthetically, it should be as easy to get a divorce as it is to get married, and as hard to get married as it is to get a divorce.

So . . .

DIVORCE IS TO . . .

Intelligence—what the marriage was to ignorance;
Maturity—what the marriage was to immaturity;
Self-reliance—what the marriage was to dependency;
Confrontation—what the marriage was to avoidance;
Reality—what the marriage was to illusion;
Courage—what the marriage was to fear;
Love—what the marriage was to infatuation;
A beginning—what the marriage was to an end.